Instructor's Manual

Mosaic 1

Reading

4th Edition

Prepared by

Janet Podnecky

McGraw-Hill Contemporary

McGraw-Hill/Contemporary
A Division of The McGraw-Hill Companies

Mosaic 1 Reading Instructor's Manual, 4th Edition

Published by McGraw-Hill/Contemporary, a business unit of The McGraw-Hill Companies, Inc., 1221 Avenue of the Americas, New York, NY 10020. Copyright © 2002, 1996, 1990, 1985 by The McGraw-Hill Companies, Inc. All rights reserved. No part of this publication may be reproduced or distributed in any form or by any means, or stored in a database or retrieval system, without the prior written consent of The McGraw-Hill Companies, Inc., including, but not limited to, in any network or other electronic storage or transmission, or broadcast for distance learning.

 This book is printed on recycled, acid-free paper containing 10% postconsumer waste.

1 2 3 4 5 6 7 8 9 0 QPD/QPD 0 9 8 7 6 5 4 3 2 1

ISBN 0-07-248146-3

Editorial director: *Tina B. Carver*
Series editor: *Annie Sullivan*
Development editors: *Louis Carrillo, Annie Sullivan*
Director of marketing: *Thomas P. Dare*
Production and composition: *A Good Thing, Inc.*
Printer: *Phoenix Color*

www.mhcontemporary.com/interactionsmosaic

TABLE OF CONTENTS

Introduction

Mosaic 1 Reading encourages students to become actively involved in their own reading development. Students' thoughts and input are crucial in the reading process. They need to form ideas before reading a selection, pick out important ideas as they read, and finally, consider and discuss critically the main idea—the writer's message. The students are interacting with the reading selections, with the writers' ideas, and with others in the class.

The goal of **Mosaic 1 Reading** is for students to become independent readers through instruction in the various reading skills and through intensive and extensive readings. There are pre- and post-reading exercises to develop reading skills and vocabulary. The exercises carefully introduce and model the key skills. Expansion and extension ideas provide additional challenging work to meet the individual needs of more advanced learners.

The reading level is challenging. The selections represent the different learning fields in order to prepare students to use academic textbooks. Students practice identifying main ideas, organizing information, interpreting ideas, and preparing summaries—skills needed for academic study and research. Although technical vocabulary may be pre-taught, students are encouraged to use context clues to infer meanings of new vocabulary. Sentence structures include complex and compound sentences that are common in academic texts. Finally, the reading passages express various cultural viewpoints and issues for analysis and class discussion.

General Teaching Suggestions

Teacher's Role

The reading teacher has a multi-faceted role. At times, the teacher needs to give instruction especially about language issues and provide cultural and background information that is important to the topic. Other times, the teacher is a participant listening to and sharing opinions and taking part in class and group discussions. The teacher is also a facilitator, creating a classroom environment that promotes learning and communication. Finally, the teacher provides encouragement and feedback, challenging students to continue developing their reading skills.

Teaching Practices

As your role as teacher changes in the classroom, you will want to adjust the practices you use. With whole class activities, such as large group discussions and sharing of ideas, initial presentations, and comprehension activities, you need to keep students' attention.

- Use volunteers as models and then call on others in the class.
- List important information and words on the board.
- Maintain a lively pace in the class.
- Try to give everyone a chance to participate.

When checking comprehension of reading selections, begin with *yes/no* questions and *or-* questions, allowing the beginning level students to answer. Then ask information questions (*wh-* questions: *who, what, when, where, why*). Later, ask questions to the more advanced students that require more critical and creative thinking. These would be questions that involve analyzing, making inferences, and making comparisons. For example: *What would you suggest …? How do you ….? Why would someone …?* As you go through the reading selections, you may want to stop after each paragraph to check understanding and to point out and discuss key vocabulary words.

As you review the responses to the student book exercises, ask volunteers to explain their answers and to justify their responses. If appropriate, have the class look back at the readings to verify information and details. In exercises where more than one answer is possible, invite several students to share their responses and ideas.

Groupwork

Small groups allow students more of a chance to participate in discussion activities. It is often easier to speak in a small group than in front of the whole class, so the small group situation is more secure for those who are less proficient in their speaking skills. In addition, it allows time for students to help each other with vocabulary. Students can think and practice saying something in a small group before addressing a larger audience. Group work promotes discussion and sharing of ideas and cultural understanding. Students can learn from each other. Group work also allows you to address individual needs of students

When students are working in groups, be sure that:

- students understand the directions of the activity
- everyone in the group is involved or has a role
- students show respect for each other
- there is a time limit for the activity
- groups have a chance to share what they discussed or prepared.

Divide the class into groups of 4 – 6 for discussions and group writing activities. Prepare for groupwork. Have the following roles clearly defined for each member of the group:

- *reader,* or *facilitator,* who reads instructions, guides the group, is the leader
- *recorder,* who takes notes on discussions and answers for the activity
- *checker,* who makes sure everyone in the group understands points and watches the time, etc.
- *reporter,* who will share the group's information with the rest of the class

As groups are working, go around the room listening. You may need to assist with vocabulary or give other guidance. Your job is to facilitate the group activity, not to lead it. Make a note of types of problems that arise and address them later.

Vocabulary

Before each of the reading selections, students discuss what they already know about a topic area. Basic vocabulary is sometimes reviewed or presented in illustrations and in pre-reading questions. Make a list of words for students to refer to as they work through the chapter. Encourage students to make general

guesses about the meanings of the new words based on the context clues. Later, they may want to check a dictionary for the precise meanings.

Multi-level Classes

Students have different needs and learning styles, so there will usually be a range of levels within a class. By varying the types of activities, you can address the needs of all students. Use whole class activities for presenting and modeling activities. Allow students to work individually, in pairs, or small groups to practice and prepare responses. During this time, give individual attention as needed. Have students work together in cooperative groups, not competitive groups. In this way, all students will participate, contribute, help, and learn from each other rather than competing against each other. You may want to provide additional reading materials for these advanced learners to browse through if they finish earlier than others. If possible, allow students to explore the Internet for related readings and information to share with the class related to the chapter topics.

You may want to ask students to evaluate their own progress halfway through the course. Ask them to write down if they feel they are making progress and what they feel they have learned so far in the course. Also ask them to write down what they hope to achieve in the second half of the course and how you can best help them achieve their goals. As you read through their self-evaluations, make notes about common goals they have to incorporate into the course. Give students feedback on their progress, too.

Using the Video

The video component provides additional activities related to the chapter topics. Each segment presents some culturally significant concept, fact, or issue. You may choose to use the video at the end of the chapter, as a culminating activity that reinforces listening, speaking, reading, and writing skills. The video section may be used at the beginning of a chapter to present the basic content area and initiate discussion of the basic content. Alternatively, you might find it more appropriate to use the video section to break up the heavy reading content and reading skills exercises in the chapter.

For each video segment there are several activities. The first exercise prepares students for watching the video. Students list vocabulary or share information that they know about the topic. They can make predictions about what they will see based on the title and the activity questions. The next two activities guide students as they watch the video at least two times. Students should read the questions before watching so they will know what information they need to find. The video segments are relatively short, so students are encouraged to watch the videos several times. The final video exercise invites students to check for other information related to the video segment in newspapers, magazines, and on the Internet. It leads students to read for information and to apply their reading skills to things outside of the classroom.

Administering the Reading Placement Test

The Reading Placement test helps teachers and administrators place students into the Reading strand of the **Interactions Mosaic** series. All of the placement tests have been carefully designed to assess a student's language proficiency as it correlates to the different levels of the **Interactions Mosaic** series.

The Reading test has been created to assess both vocabulary development skills and reading comprehension skills. The first three parts of the test assess the skills students use to determine word meaning. Part 1 focuses on determining meaning and usage from context. Part 2 narrows in on idiomatic expressions. Part 3 determines whether students can scan for members of word families. The final part of the test, Part 4, assesses reading comprehension and consists of four different reading selections. The selections vary in length and complexity. Students must answer both literal and inferential questions.

The tests follow multiple choice and true/false formats for easy administration and scoring. Use the following charts to place your students in the correct level of text. To maintain test validity, be sure to collect all copies of the test and store the test in a secure location.

Placement Chart for the Reading Test

Number of Items Correct	Place in
0–10	Needs a more basic text.
11–17	Interactions Access
18–24	Interactions 1
25–34	Interactions 2
36–43	Mosaic 1
43–48	Mosaic 2

Using the Chapter Quizzes

The **Mosaic 1 Reading** quizzes allow teachers to assess whether the students have mastered the vocabulary and basic comprehension of the reading passages in the chapters. In addition, they help assess how well students can use the language to communicate in writing their own ideas and thoughts about the chapter topics.

The **Mosaic 1 Reading** quizzes do not test students' reading comprehension or summarizing skills. The teacher should be assessing and evaluating students' reading skills as they complete the exercises in the chapters.

The chapter quizzes also bring closure to chapters and give students a feeling of achievement and progress as they go through the textbook and course.

Description

There are 12 quizzes, one for each chapter in the reading text. Each quiz contains five sections:

- vocabulary
- comprehension: Part 1
- comprehension: Part 2
- grammar/structure
- self-expression

The first section checks students' understanding of key vocabulary about the chapter topics. The vocabulary items are selected from the first two reading selections of the chapter. Students match the words with their meanings or synonyms.

The comprehension sections check general understanding of the key ideas of the main reading selections of the chapter. The ideas are about the main ideas rather than specific details from the readings. Students decide if statements are true or false or identify key characters or features of the readings.

A major grammar or language structure for each chapter is highlighted in the fourth section of the quizzes. Students choose the correct word form to complete sentences. Some of the structures tested are: verb tense forms, pronouns, related words (nouns, verbs, and adjectives), and words with similar meanings. Although there are no exercises in the student book on these specific grammar points, students need to use them throughout the chapter exercises.

The last section allows students to write their own personal views and responses to questions related to the chapter topics. The questions give students a chance to reflect on their own experiences and feelings about the chapter topic. Answers will vary from student to student.

Administration

The quizzes can be duplicated and given to students individually or for full-class administration.

Scoring and Grading

Each section of the quiz is worth a specific number of points. The total possible score is 25 points.

New Challenges

Goals

- **Use context clues**
- **Recall main ideas and important details**
- **Analyze topic sentences**
- **Understand suffixes:** *-able, -al, -ant, -er, -ity, -less, -ation, -ful, -ment, -ous*
- **Understand combination words**
- **Talk about preferences in housing**
- **Find implied main ideas**
- **Understand prefixes:** *non-, anti-*
- **Analyze points of contrast**

Part 1 Living in the U.S.A.

Introduce the chapter topic by reading together the **In This Chapter** note on page 1. Allow volunteers to share information and misinformation they know about the United States and Canada. Guide discussion of experiences students have had with Americans and Canadians. You may want to make a list of students' ideas and views for review later at the end of the chapter.

Before You Read

1 **Reading Without Knowing the Meaning of Every Word. Page 2.**
Read together the information and tips. Guide students as they look over the article and follow the first suggestion. Point out sub-headings and illustrations as needed. Encourage volunteers to suggest what the article will be about. Explain

that students will listen to the audiocassette as they read which will allow them to focus on the main ideas in the second step. Later, they will check their understanding as described in the third step.

Read

Living in the U.S.A. Page 2. [on tape/CD]
Play the tape or CD as students follow along in their books. You may want to stop the recording after every section to check understanding and point out important vocabulary. Listen a second time as students read along.

After You Read

2 **Recalling Information. Page 4.**
Read the instructions and have students complete the exercise. Then discuss the answers with the whole class.

Answers: 1. T 2. F 3. F 4. F 5. T 6. T 7. F 8. T 9. F

Ask students to point out the information that is not true in the false statements. Students can look back in the reading selection for the correct information. Have volunteers restate the false statements to make them true.

3 **Analyzing Topic Sentences. Page 4.**
As you read aloud the explanation, be sure students understand "main idea" and "supporting sentences" or "details." Tell students to use the information from the explanation as they answer the questions about topic sentences. Have students work with partners. Then go over the answers with the group.

Answers: 1. True 2. a 3. b 4. exclamation point; Houses interest Americans greatly.

Chapter 1

4 Getting the Meaning of Words from Context. Page 5.

Read together the instructions about using context clues. Model using context clues to guess the meaning of "blunt." Then have students look back at the reading selection for the contexts of the other vocabulary words in the exercise. After students have made their guesses, go over the answers. Encourage students to explain how they made their choices.

Answers: 2. c 3. a 4. a 5. c 6. b 7. b 8. b 9. a

5 Six Useful Suffixes. Page 5.

Read together the instructions. You may want to have students suggest examples of nouns, verbs, and adjectives. Discuss their functions in sentences as needed. Point out the six suffixes and go over the first suffix and sample words. Then have students complete the rest of the exercise filling in words with the suffixes. Go over the suffixes and new words. Have students suggest other words that contain these suffixes.

Answers: seasonal, applicant, teacher, cordiality, harmless

6 Making New Words by Adding Suffixes. Page 6.

Go over the instructions together. After students have completed the exercise, go over the answers. Point out spelling rules as needed.

Answers: 2. gardener 3. driver 4. comfortable 5. formality 6. informality 7. inhabitant 8. acceptable 9. occasional 10. desirable 11. personal 12. responsibility 13. restless 14. continental 15. brevity 16. nationality

7 Getting the Meaning of Combination Words. Page 6.

Read together the instructions and example. Then have students complete the exercise individually. Go over the answers with the group.

Sample Answers: 2. a list of things to do
3. books that teach you to help yourself
4. a person who does good things

Around the Globe

This activity allows students to compare and contrast cultural customs in the United States and in their own countries. Students work with partners reading about American customs and answering the questions about the pictures. As students work, go around the room listening and giving assistance as needed. When students have finished the exercise, invite volunteers to share their answers and most interesting information from their discussions.

Answers: 1 - 3 Answers will vary. Questions 2, 4, 6, and 8 are generally considered impolite in American culture.

8 Talking About Preferences. Page 9.

In this activity, students express their own personal preferences about customs and content mentioned in the reading selection. Arrange students in groups of four for discuss each of the customs and attitudes. Ask volunteers from each group to summarize their preferences.

Talk It Over

This activity allows students to talk about their own cultural perspectives and experiences related to American customs. Arrange students in groups of four. Give the groups about 15-20 minutes to discuss the questions. Circulate among the groups, listening, and giving assistance as need. When all groups are finished, ask volunteers from each group to share the most interesting information and ideas from their groups.

Answers will vary.

Part 2 My Country

Before You Read

1 Getting the Meaning of Words from Context and Structure. Page 10.
Read aloud the directions and go over the example together. If needed, use the exercise on page 5 to review using context clues to guess meanings. After students complete the exercise, go over the answers together.

Answers: 2. large size 3. looks around 4. character 5. similar 6. wetness 7. has just arrived 8. small battles 9. sheriffs and policemen 10. shy 11. in the French way 12. who have the same nationality as I do

Read

2 Finding Implied Main Ideas. Page 10.
Read together the instructions and go over carefully the first paragraph and example. Then, have students work individually reading the paragraphs and identifying the topics and topic sentences. Before going over the answers, you may want to read aloud the paragraphs again, pausing to ask comprehension questions and pointing out key vocabulary. Ask volunteers to identify the main idea of each of the paragraphs.

Answers: 2. c 3. b 4. a 5. c

After You Read

3 Comprehending the Reading. Page 14.
Have students complete the exercise, referring back to the reading selection as needed. Go over the answers with the class.

Answers: 1. F 2. T 3. F 4. F 5. T 6. F 7. F 8. T 9. F 10. F

4 Words With the Prefixes *anti-* and *non-*. Page 14.
Read the explanation of the prefixes and their meanings. Call attention to the examples before having students complete the exercise. After you go over the answers with the class, ask students to suggest other words that contain these prefixes. Discuss the meanings of these words.

Sample Answers: 3. protest against war 4. a group that is not violent 5. people who are not Germans 6. people who are not Mexicans 7. people who are against communists 8. people who don't vote 9. laws against monopolies 10. payment that was not made

5 Four More Suffixes. Page 15.
Point out the new suffixes and their meanings. Have volunteers identify the first example in each of the items. Have students use the suffixes to create other words to complete the exercise. Go over the answers together.

Answers: 1. decoration 2. harmful 3. government 4. glorious

6 Making New Words by Adding Suffixes. Page 15.
Review the suffixes from Exercise 5. Then have students find words that contain the suffixes in the reading to complete the sentences. Check the answers together.

Answers: 2. imagination 3. powerful 4. moderation 5. settlement 6. mountainous 7. movement 8. mysterious

Talk It Over

This activity gives students a chance to express their own opinions and feelings related to ideas in the reading. Arrange students in groups of four or five to talk about their own thoughts on the national character and culture. Allow 15-20 minutes for discussion. Allow time for groups to report their ideas.

Sample Answers:

1. Canada, Bahamas, Barbados, Belize, Dominica, Grenada, Guyana, Jamaica, St. Kitts-Nevis, Saint-Lucia, St. Vincent and the Grenadines, Trinidad and Tobago all separated in non-violent ways from England. Suriname separated from the Netherlands. Answers will vary.

2. Quebec is the only province that is predominately French-speaking.

3. There are two official languages. Answers will vary.

4. & 5. Answers will vary.

Focus on Testing

Analyzing Points of Contrast

In each chapter, there is a section to help students develop and refine their test-taking skills. This section encourages students to notice types tests and test questions and gives students tips on how to respond to them. Remind students that the information and tips in this section will help prepare them for tests in other academic areas.

Read together the instructions, clarifying as needed. Then have students read the paragraph and complete the exercise. Then arrange students in pairs to discuss their answers. Go over the answers with the whole class.

Answers: 1. American 2. Canadian
3. Canadian 4. American 5. American
6. Canadian 7. American 8. Canadian
9. Canadian 10. American

What Do You Think?

Panhandling

This part of the chapter provides additional discussion questions related to the chapter topic.

You may want to read together this section before arranging students in group for discussion. As students work in small groups, go around giving assistance as needed. After 10-15 minutes of discussion, have volunteers report to the class the most interesting points of their discussions.

Answers will vary.

Video Activities: An Exchange Student

Before You Watch

Read the questions aloud and ask students to discuss their answers in small groups. Have students report to the class their answers.

Sample Answers: 1. An exchange student is a usually a high school student who goes to a school in a foreign country for a period of time, living with a local family and attending a local high school. 2. Some problems that exchange students might have are the language, the local customs, eating habits and types of foods, homesickness, and personality conflicts.

Watch [on video]

Ask students to read the questions to prepare them for the video. Then play the video and have them answer the questions. Review the answers together.

Answers: 1. c 2. d 3. a 4. a 5. c

Watch Again [on video]

Point out the questions and explain that students need to watch carefully to find the answers. Replay the video and have students complete the exercise. Go over the answers with the whole class to summarize the information.

Answers: 1. 18 years old 2. b 3. a. English and French b. physics c. A 4. c 5. c

After You Watch

Assign this for homework. Remind students to use the information about suffixes from this lesson as they try to guess the meanings of the words they find. Allow time for students to share their lists of words.

Answers will vary.

Looking at Learning

Goals

- **Scan for slang words and expressions**
- **Recognize characteristics of informal style**
- **Select the main idea**
- **Understand prefixes: *pre-, re-, un-***
- **Make new words by adding prefixes**
- **Describe a person**
- **Use clustering for speed and comprehension**
- **Get the meaning of words from context**
- **Take objective tests**
- **Scan for specific information**

Part 1 How To Read Faster

Use the information in **In This Chapter** note on page 19 to introduce the chapter topic. Ask volunteers to describe reading and test-taking techniques they use.

Before You Read

1 **Scanning for Slang Words and Expressions. Page 20.**
Read together about slang words and scanning. Ask students to scan for the specific slang words used in the reading on pages 21-22. Go over the answers. Encourage students to point out which of the slang words they have heard before and where they have heard them.

Answers: 1. kid 2. zipped 3. a snap 4. eyeballs 5. chicken 6. beat it

Then introduce the reading by sharing the background information about the author.

2 **Characteristics of Informal Style. Page 20.**
Have students look over the reading selection again to find the answers to the questions about informal style. As you go over the answers, have volunteers point out examples from the reading that support their answers.

Sample Answers:
1. Short paragraphs
2. Short sentences
3. A
4. Yes. "In addition to contracts, novels, and newspapers; screenplays, tax returns, and correspondence. Even textbooks about how people read. And which techniques help people read more in less time." "And let you cut out an awful lot of unnecessary reading."
5. The style is personal because the author is talking a lot about himself (I) and addresses the reader as "you." There are a lot of expressions that you usually hear in coversation like "mind you" and "Ready?"

Read

How to Read Faster. Page 21.
Read the selection as students follow along in their books. You may want to stop after every section to check understanding and point out important vocabulary words. Read a second time as students follow along.

After You Read

3 **Selecting the Main Idea. Page 24.**
Review main idea by reading the explanation and exercise instructions. After students make their selection, discuss the answer. Encourage

volunteers to explain why the other choices are not good main ideas for this reading.

Answer: 2

4 More Prefixes. Page 24.

Call attention to the new prefixes: *pre-, re-, and un-*. Remind students that prefixes are added to the beginning of words to change the meanings of the words. Have students use the information about the prefixes to complete definitions about some words. Go over the answers with the group.

Answers: 2. to look over something again 3. to read it again 4. material that is not familiar 5. reading that is not needed or necessary

Have students use the words with prefixes in their own sentences or find examples of other words with the same prefixes to share with the class.

5 Making New Words by Adding Prefixes. Page 24.

Go over the instructions and example together. After students have completed the exercise, go over the answers.

Answers: 2. precook 3. uncooperative 4. redo 5. preschool 6. unaware 7. rerun 8. pregame 9. unappreciative

Talk It Over

Arrange students in groups of four to summarize and restate information from the article to answer the questions. Give the groups about 15-20 minutes to discuss the questions. Circulate among the groups, listening, and giving assistance as need. When all groups are finished, ask volunteers from each group to share their responses.

Sample Answers:

1. Previewing is a useful technique for long, difficult readings. It gives you a general idea of the reading in a short time.

2. You can preview eight to ten 100-page reports in an hour.

3. To preview, you read the first couple of paragraphs. Then you read the first sentence in the other paragraphs. Finally, you read the whole last two paragraphs.

4. It's better to skim when you're reviewing something you have read before or when you're looking at light, easy reading, such as magazines, sports and entertainment sections of the newspaper.

5. To skim, you look across the lines and pick out and "read" the key words in each line.

6. Clustering is better for fast reading when you need to understand most of the material. It helps you remember more of the information than skimming or previewing.

7. When you cluster, you group words together in logical clusters.

8. "Heavy" reading is academic reading as in textbooks and journal articles. "Light" reading is reading you might do for relaxing or something that is not important to remember. It's reading for enjoyment as in magazine and newspaper articles.

6 Adjectives That Describe a Person. Page 25.

Go over the instructions and list of words on the chart. Students can look up words in the dictionary as needed. Allow 5 minutes for students to work in pairs marking the adjectives. As you go over the answers, have volunteers point out information or passages from the reading selection that support the responses.

Sample Answers:

N: arrogant, unpleasant, negative, snobbish

Y: effective, humorous, serious, competent, good-natured, well-educated

7 Small Group Discussion. Page 25.
You may want to allow time for students to choose one of the topics and prepare some notes for their informal talks. Then arrange students in groups of four or five to present their talks. As students work, go around the room listening and giving assistance as needed. Encourage students to ask each other questions. After students have completed their talks, guide discussion of their experiences. *What was easy about giving the talk? What was difficult? What types of expressions were often used in the informal talks? When might you need to give an informal talk?*

Timed Reading

Using Clustering for Speed and Comprehension

This activity allows students to apply one of the reading techniques from Part 1. Read the instructions for the activity. Review clustering as needed. Call attention to the Comprehension Quiz on pages 27-28. Remind students to look over the questions beforehand to guide their reading of the encyclopedia article. Then have students read the article and complete the quiz. Go over the answers.

Answers: 1. b 2. b 3. a 4. b 5. c 6. a 7. c 8. c 9. a 10. c

What Do You Think?

In this activity, students discuss their views on censorship. Read together the introductory material on reasons some people want censorship. Then arrange students in groups of four for discuss their views on the topic. Ask volunteers from each group to summarize their groups' views on censorship.

Part 2 How to Take Tests

Before You Read

1 Getting the Meaning of Words from Context. Page 29.
Read aloud the directions, reviewing context clues as needed. After students complete the exercise, go over the answers together.

Answers: 1. d 2. b 3. c 4. a 5. d 6. d 7. a 8. b 9. a

Read

How to Take Tests: Scoring What You're Worth. Page 31.
Use the introductory material to present the reading selection. Have students find the section headings and make predications about the content. Then have students read the selection.

After You Read

2 Scanning for Specific Information. Page 32.
Have students complete the exercise, referring back to the reading selection as needed. Go over the answers with the class.

Answers: 1. objective 2. usually, rarely, sometimes 3. true 4. read the answers first 5. two of the above, none of the above 6. first 7. length, number 8. outline 9. background conclusion 10. invent your own question

Talk It Over

Students can discuss their answers to the questions on test-taking experiences and the advice from the reading selection. Arrange students in groups of four or five to talk about their own experiences on testing. Allow 15-20 minutes for discussion. Ask volunteers from each group to summarize their ideas and most interesting views.

Answers will vary.

Focus on Testing

Taking an Objective Test
Read together the suggestions, clarifying as needed.

Sample Test of Reading Comprehension
Read aloud the instructions, clarifying as needed. Call attention to the places for recording answers. Remind students of the test-taking suggestions they read about. Then have students complete the exercise. Have students check their own work. Discuss any difficulties they encountered.

Answers: 1. b 2. c 3. b 4. d 5. c 6. c 7. a 8. b 9. a 10. d

Video Activities: High-Tech Jobs and Low-Tech People

Before You Watch
Read the questions aloud and ask students to discuss their answers in small groups. Have students report to the class their answers.

Answers: 1. b, d 2. c

Watch [on video]
Ask students to read the questions to prepare them for the video. Then play the video and have them answer the questions. Review the answers together.

Answers: 1. b 2. c 3. c 4. b, d, e

Watch Again [on video]
Point out the questions and explain that students need to watch carefully to find the answers. Replay the video and have students complete the exercise. Go over the answers with the whole class to summarize the information.

Answers: 1. a, b 2. Manpower Inc.
3. a. a place to work, b. certain degree, to do something cool

After You Watch
Assign this for homework. Remind students that clustering takes practice. They can do this type of activity periodically to check their own reading speed and accuracy.

Chapter 3

Relationships

Goals

- Skim for the general idea
- Recall information
- Read a statistical chart
- Talk about child care
- Scan for facts
- Identify general and specific statements
- Eliminate the incorrect choices
- Select the main idea
- Understand real-life reading: personals section
- Discuss adoption policies

Part 1 Who's Taking Care of the Children?

Read together **In This Chapter** note on page 39. Guide discussion of family relationships and childcare options that students know. Review basic vocabulary for the chapter.

Before You Read

1 **Skimming for the General Idea. Page 40.**
Present the information on skimming for the general idea in the exercise instructions. Review skimming from Chapter 2 as needed. Then have students skim the article and circle the best summary. As you go over the answer, ask volunteers to explain why the other choices are not good answers.

Answer: 2

Read

2 **Who's Taking Care of the Children? Page 40. [on tape/CD]**
Play the tape or CD as students follow along in their books. You may want to stop the recording after every section to check understanding and point out important vocabulary words. Listen again and have students reread the selection.

After You Read

3 **Matching Words to Their Definitions. Page 42.**
Read the instructions and have students complete the exercise. Remind students to use context clues in the reading instead of a dictionary to help match the words and definitions. Review the answers with the whole class.

Answers: 1. c 2. i 3. e 4. g 5. a 6. h 7. b 8. j 9. k 10. l 11. f 12. d

As an extension activity, have students use the vocabulary words in sentences.

4 **Recalling Information. Page 42.**
Students can check back in the reading selection to verify their answers.

Answers: 1. 70 2. stay-at-home mom 3. nuclear 4. larger cities 5. more

5 **Reading a Statistical Chart. Page 43.**
Introduce the exercise by reading together the information about statistical charts. If needed, call attention to the labels on the chart. Students can work individually or in pairs to answer the questions about American family changes based on the statistics. Go over the answers with the group.

Answers:
1. The chart shows changes in the types of American families by ethnicity.

2. The percentage went down.
3. In 1980.
4. The years that showed no change were 1992, -3, 1994, -5, and 1996-98.
5. The percentage went up.
6. The percentage went up.
7. The percentage of 2-parent families decreased; the percentage of 1-parent families increased.

Talk It Over

Encourage students to use the information they have ready about in this chapter and their own personal experiences and values as they discuss the questions with group members. Allow about 15-20 minutes to discuss the questions. Remind students that they do not need to agree on their answers, but they should give information to support their answers. Circulate among the groups, listening, and giving assistance as need. When all groups are finished, ask volunteers from each group to share the most interesting information and ideas from their groups.

Answers will vary.

Part 2 70 Brides for 7 Foreigners

Before You Read

1 **Scanning for Facts. Page 45.**
After reading together the instructions, read the items and the introductory paragraph. Have students make predictions about the selection. Then have students scan the selection for the answers. Go over the answers together. Ask volunteers to point out lines where they found the information.

Answers: 2. Yaroslav the Wise 3. 100 4. 10 5. 5% 6. United States, Germany, Britain 7. 1,200

Read

Have students reread the article.

After You Read

2 **Identifying General and Specific Statements. Page 48.**
As you read together the instructions, clarify "general" and "specific" statements. Have volunteers suggest ways to distinguish them. Guide students to identify the types of statements that are in the exercise columns. Then have students match the specific and the general statements. Go over the answers with the group.

Answers: First column: Specific statements
Second column: General statements
1. b 2. e 3. a 4. d 5. c

3 **Selecting the Main Idea. Page 48.**
Review "main idea" if necessary. Then have students choose the best statement. As you go over the answer, ask volunteers to explain why the other statements are not good statements of main idea.

Answer: 2

Talk It Over

Students have a chance to express their own opinions and feelings related to relationships. Arrange students in groups of four or five to talk about their own thoughts on the relationship questions. Allow 15-20 minutes for discussion. Allow time for groups to report their ideas.

Sample Answers:
1. The mother of the man from Sydney thinks that Australian women don't make good wives. They are too independent and liberated, so they don't take good care of the house and their husbands. She probably sees and hears a lot from people around or in the news.

2. & 3. Answers will vary.

4. The criteria for the dating agency is good because the people must be serious. The

people on file are paying so they want to have some good possibilities if a match is made. It's not completely fair.

5. I would consider marrying someone from a different culture. The advantages might be more opportunities for children to learn languages and about the world. The disadvantages might be different ideas and values in terms of raising children, family roles, traditions, and acceptable behavior.

6. There have always been some people that don't marry. It depends on the reason why the people make that decision: for religious dedication, for professional or career advancement, for lack of respect for cultural norms. I think marriage shows the commitment that people have towards each other, the family unit, and the general society. For those that choose not to marry, they may change their minds later in life.

4 Real-life Reading. Page 49.

Assign the exercise as homework. When students bring in their ads, have them compare them and talk about the answers to the questions. Allow time for students to draft and written opinion about the ads to share with the class.

Answers will vary.

What Do You Think?

Adoption

Read the introductory material about adoption. Go over vocabulary as needed. You may want to have students work with partners to prepare their responses to the questions. Remind them to check back in the other chapter readings for criteria and qualifications for other agencies. Invite volunteers to share with the class their lists of qualifications. Help summarize the responses.

Focus on Testing

Eliminating the Incorrect Choices

Read together the instructions, calling attention to the common pattern of multiple choice answers. Help students identify the different categories in the example test question. Then have students complete the exercise. Arrange students in pairs to compare their answers. Go over the answers with the whole class, asking volunteers to identify examples of "decoys", completely wrong or opposites, and close in meaning choices.

Answers: 1. a 2. a 3. b 4. c 5. b

Video Activities: True Love

Before You Watch

Have students rank the causes from most common to least common. Have volunteers report to the class their orders and explain their reasoning.

Sample Answers: 5, 1, 3, 4, 2

Watch [on video]

Ask students to read the questions to prepare them for the video. Then play the video and have them answer the questions. Review the answers together.

Answers: 1. c 2. c 3. a, d 4. b 5. c

Watch Again [on video]

Point out the questions and explain that students need to watch carefully to find the answers. Replay the video and have students complete the exercise. After students compare their answers in small groups, review their responses.

Answers:

1. b, d, e, f
2. a
3. 1. b 2. c 3. a

After You Watch

Assign this for homework. Remind students to check back in Chapter 2 to review skimming. Have students share their articles with partners or in small groups.

Answers will vary.

Chapter 4

Health and Leisure

Goals

- **Use headings as guides**
- **Get the meaning of words from context**
- **Recall information**
- **Formulate the key ideas**
- **Understand specialized use of vocabulary**
- **Analyze compound words**
- **Skim for the point of view**
- **Separate fact from opinion**
- **Scan for vocabulary**
- **Discuss healthy diets and tourism**
- **Brainstorm**
- **Support a position**
- **Scan charts**

Part 1 Eat Like a Peasant, Feel Like a King

Introduce the chapter topic by reading together the **In This Chapter** note on page 53. Ask volunteers to share things they eat and do to stay healthy.

Before You Read

1 Using Headings as Guides. Page 54.

Ask students to look over the article and find the headings. After they have written the headings in the spaces, read together about the kinds of headings. Have students complete the questions about the headings in this article. Discuss the answers with the group.

Answers:

2. Early Diets: Nuts and Plants
3. Why Socrates Loved Olive Oil
4. Healthy Diets Around the World
   - 2 and 4 tell the main topic of the section.
   - Section 2 will probably be about foods that people ate in early civilizations. Section 3 might be about the diet of Greek and people in the Mediterranean area. Section 4 may be about healthy foods and dishes from around the world.

2 Getting the Meaning of Words from Context. Page 54.

Review using context clues to guess the meanings of unfamiliar words. Model the first item as needed. Students can work in pairs to complete the exercise. Go over the answers.

Sample Answers:

1. *A peasant diet* is probably food that poor working people eat. The title implied that the simple peasant diet is better, more healthy than rich foods that the more wealthy people might eat.
2. *Elite* means people of the highest class in society.
3. *Eclectic* means using the best from various sources or of various types.
4. *Affluence* means a large supply of riches. A synonym for it is *prosperity*.
5. *Cuisine* means a style of cooking or preparing food.

Read aloud the notes at the end of the exercise. These contain some questions to guide students' reading of the following selection. Encourage volunteers to make predictions about the reading by suggesting answers to them. Remind students to think about these guiding questions as they read and listen to the selection.

Read

Eat Like a Peasant, Feel Like a King. Page 55.

Read the selection as students follow along in their books. You may want to stop after every section to check understanding and point out important vocabulary words. Read a second time as students follow along.

After You Read

3 Recalling Information. Page 59.

Have students complete the exercise. Discuss the answers with the whole class. Ask students to point out the part of the reading where they obtained the information for their answers.

Answers: 1. c 2. f 3. b 4. d 5. a 6. e

4 Formulating Key Ideas. Page 59.

Review "main idea" and "key ideas" as needed. Students can complete the exercise individually or in pairs. As you go over the answers, point out how the main idea and other key ideas are connected.

Sample Answers:

1. There are simple foods and dishes from around the world that are healthier than more expensive types of foods.

2. As people become more affluent, they begin eating differently. The new diet tends to be less healthy than the more simple foods. As Japan became more affluent, the people began eating more beef and butter (with higher cholesterol levels) and less grains and beans. The people become more overweight and developed more cases of heart disease. In India, more affluent people preferred eating foods cooked in butter and coconut oil which are high in saturated fats, so the people became more overweight.

5 Specialized Use of Vocabulary. Page 60.

Read together the instructions and example of specialized use of words. Point out that the usual definitions of the vocabulary words are explained in the exercise. Students need to use the information in the items to explain the specialized use of the words. Have students work in pairs to define the words as they are used in the reading. Go over the answers with the group.

Sample Answers:

1. The usual small eating or snacking habit is interrupted periodically by large meals or feasts after a hunt.

2. "Quaff" means to drink quickly.

Talk It Over

Arrange students in groups of four to discuss the questions about cuisines and eating habits. You may want to read together the questions first and discuss any new vocabulary. Then, give the groups about 15-20 minutes to discuss the questions. Circulate among the groups, listening, and giving assistance as need. When all groups are finished, ask volunteers from each group to share the most interesting information and ideas from their groups.

Answers will vary.

Focus on Testing

Analyzing Compound Words

This section encourages students to develop strategies for understanding compound words. Read together the instructions, clarifying as needed. Then have students read the paragraph and complete the exercise. Then arrange students in pairs to discuss their answers. Go over the answers with the whole class.

Answers: 1. b 2. d 3. c 4. c 5. a 6. c

What Do You Think?

Smoking

Read together the information on smoking. Go over vocabulary as needed. Then, arrange students in groups of four. Give the groups about 15-20 minutes to discuss the questions and the chart. As the groups work, go around the room listening and giving assistance as needed. Ask volunteers from each group to share the most interesting information and ideas from their groups.

Answers will vary.

Part 2 Here Come the Tourists!

Before You Read

1 Skimming for the Point of View. Page 63.
Read aloud the directions, clarifying "point of view." Review the purpose of skimming. After students complete the exercise, go over the answer to the question of point of view and discuss students' attitudes towards tourism.

Answers: 2. X

2 Getting the Meaning of Words from Context. Page 63.
Review using context clues as needed. Students can work with partners to complete the exercise. As you go over the answers with the group, have students explain how they decided on their responses.

Answers: 1. c 2. d 3. a; b 4. d 5. b 6. c; d 7. c; b

Read

Here Come the Tourists! Page 66. [on tape/CD]

Read together introductory paragraph about the selection and author. Then have students read along as you play the tape or CD. Stop as needed to check comprehension and vocabulary.

After You Read

3 Separating Fact from Opinion. Page 67.
Read together the information on facts and opinions. You may want to have students suggest words and expressions commonly used with facts and opinions. Have students complete the exercise, referring back to the reading selection to check contexts. Allow time for students to compare their answers with partners before going over the answers with the class. As an extension activity, have students write 2 more statements of fact and opinion based on the reading selection.

Answers: 1. F 2. F 3. O 4. O 5. F 6. F 7. F 8. O 9. F 10. F

4 Scanning for Vocabulary. Page 68.
After reading together the instructions, have students complete the exercise. Students will need to refer back to the reading selection. After you go over the answers with the class, ask students to use the words in other sentences.

Answers: 1. natural resources 2. enchanted 3. inappropriate 4. manifest 5. taboo 6. acquiring 7. flock 8. inexpensive 9. hippie 10. virtually

Talk It Over

In this activity, students consider the reading and give their personal reactions to it. Arrange students in groups of four or five for this activity. Encourage them to use the reading and their own experiences in developing their responses. Allow

15-20 minutes for discussion. Allow time for groups to report their ideas.

Sample Answers:

1. The villagers probably wanted to protect the trees, plants, and wildlife. Tourists may have come and disrupted these parts of nature. They didn't just observe and appreciate the natural resources. They wanted to touch and "play with" these things.

2. Tourism brings jobs in the hospitality industry (hotel jobs, restaurant jobs, guides). There are also jobs for interpreters, souvenir salespeople, etc. The jobs may benefit the local people by giving them jobs and financial security. But the jobs change the entire economy and life of the area. The normal jobs that supported the society before are not attractive to the local people any more. With more money in the economy, crime often becomes a problem.

3. Begging is not just a problem in developing countries. Some ways to deal with it are to provide food and shelter for the people so they don't need to beg and to prohibit "gift-giving" from tourists.

4. The woman wanted compensation for photos because the photographers sometimes use the photos for books and other money-making projects, so the people in the photos should receive some of the profit for being in the photos. Photography is taboo in some communities because they believe it hurts the people physically or spiritually.

5. I ask people before taking photos of strangers because I don't like people taking pictures of me without my permission.

6. "Budget travelers" are people that travel cheaply, on a small amount of money. They often bring money into the local economy because they don't stay at the expensive popular tourist places. They prefer to find something out-of-the-way that is less expensive. So they are in

places where more local people would stay.

7. Backpackers do not bring much money into the local economy because they tend to survive on very little, bargaining as much as possible and depending on the generosity of the local people.

8. The British bicycle tourist did not seem to have a good attitude. He was taking advantage of the people he met and didn't seem to appreciate people or things.

5 Brainstorming. Page 69.

Read together this section on brainstorming. You may want to model the activity, asking several volunteers for their suggestions for the development of the beach area. Then, have students work in pairs or small groups to brainstorm their own ideas. After 10-15 minutes, have volunteers report to the class their most interesting ideas for the developer.

Answers will vary.

6 Supporting a Position. Page 70.

Go over the instructions for the activity. Have students review bad points of tourism that were mentioned in the reading. Ask for some good points of tourism. Tell students to decide on their point of view on the impact of tourism: good, bad, or good and bad. Assign the exercise as homework. Suggest that students make a list of details or examples to support their point of view and then write their paragraph. In the next class, have students share their paragraphs with partners or in small groups.

7 Scanning Charts. Page 71.

Read together the instructions, calling attention to the two charts. Then, have students discuss and answer the question based on the charts. Go over the answer with the class.

Answer: In general, U.S. travelers do not visit the home countries of visitors to the United States in the same numbers as the visitors to the United States. In 1997, 5.3 million

Japanese visited the United States, but only 1 million U.S. tourists visited Japan. The United Kingdom has the most evenly matched numbers of reciprocal visitors: 3.7 million travelers from the United Kingdom visited the United States in 1997, and 2.9 million travelers from the United States visited the United Kingdom.

Video Activities: Bottled Water

Before You Watch
Read the questions aloud and ask students to discuss their answers in small groups. Have students report to the class their answers.

Answers:
1. Answers will vary.
2. a. T b. B c. B d. T

Watch [on video]
Ask students to read the questions to prepare them for the video. Then play the video and have them answer the questions. Review the answers together.

Answers: 1. b 2. a 3. a 4. c

Watch Again [on video]
Call attention to the questions and explain that students need to watch carefully to find the answers. Replay the video and have students complete the exercise. Go over the answers with the whole class to summarize the information.

Answers: 1. d, c 2. a. 4 b. 103 c. 1,000 d. 25% e. 1/3

After You Watch
Assign this for homework. Allow time for students to share their lists of words with others in the class.

Answers will vary

High Tech, Low Tech

Goals

- Skim for the general idea
- Make inferences about vocabulary
- Figure out the meaning of compound words
- Identify support for ideas
- Recognize colorful verbs
- Make inferences about the audience
- Write a paragraph with supporting examples
- Identify the pattern of organization
- Add suffixes to form nouns and adjectives
- Do a street interview
- Understand computerized testing

Part 1 Wired World Leaves Millions Out of the Loop

Introduce the chapter topic by reading together the **In This Chapter** note on page 73. Allow volunteers to share experiences and views on technology and its impact on the world. You may want to make a list of students' ideas and views for review later at the end of the chapter.

Before You Read

1 Skimming for the General Idea. Page 74.

Read together the information and tips about skimming. Remind students that the purpose of skimming is to get a general idea of the article. After students skim through the selection, discuss their choice of the general idea. Ask volunteers to explain why the other choices are not statements of the general idea.

Answer: c

2 Making Inferences about Vocabulary. Page 74.

Review making inferences using the information in the directions. Call attention to the example. Have volunteers explain how the meaning of "left out of the loop" was derived. Then have student work with partners to infer the meanings of the other words and expressions. Go over the answers. Discuss variations in responses.

Sample Answers:

2. There is a space between the group of people that have technology and the group that doesn't have technology. It is hard for people without to get across the space or become part of the group that has technology.

3. If we take something for granted, it means we don't realize or appreciate the value of something.

4. A "virtual university" is a university that is available through the Internet or computer technology. It is real through the computer.

3 Figuring Out the Meaning of Compound Words. Page 75.

Review the information on page 6 about compound words. Have volunteers suggest some examples. Go over the instructions for the exercise. After students complete the exercise, have them compare their answers with partners. Discuss the answers to the exercise.

Answers: 1. b 2. a 3. b 4. b 5. d 6. d 7. c 8. c

Read

Wired World Leaves Millions Out of the Loop. Page 76.

Read together the introductory paragraph before the reading. Remind students to think about the "technological gap" and how it divides the world as they listen and read the article. Read the selection as students follow along in their books. You may want to stop occasionally to check understanding and point out vocabulary words. Read a second time as students follow along.

After You Read

4 Identifying Support for Ideas. Page 78.

Read the instructions and have students complete the exercise. Point out that there is more than one detail for each of the general ideas. Discuss the answers with the whole class. Have volunteers explain how the details support the general ideas.

Sample Answers:
1. B, C, F, I
2. D, H
3. A, G, I, J, K
4. B, E, K

5 Colorful Verbs. Page 79.

Read aloud the explanation and call attention to the example. Students can work with partners to complete the exercise. Go over the answers together. Students can use the colorful verbs in their own sentences.

Answers: 2. vault 3. announced
4. dwarfed 5. bridging 6. tumbled
7. springing up

6 Making Inferences About the Audience. Page 79.

Review making inferences. Go over the directions and information about audience. Clarify as needed, pointing out the example. Then have students make other inferences about the audience by

completing the exercise. As you go over the answers, have volunteers explain their reasoning.

Answers: 2. No 3. Yes

Talk It Over

Students discuss their own opinions and views on e-mail and Internet technology. Arrange students in groups of four. Give the groups about 15-20 minutes to discuss the questions. Circulate among the groups, listening, and giving assistance as need. When all groups are finished, ask volunteers from each group to share the most interesting information and ideas from their group discussions.

Answers will vary.

7 Paragraphs With Supporting Examples. Page 80.

Use the description and the example to clarify the use of examples to support a general idea. Call attention to the restatement of the general idea. Have students underline or highlight the examples that support the general idea. Then have students state the general ideas and find the supporting examples in the other two paragraphs. Students can compare their answers with partners. Go over the answers, asking volunteers to point out the examples in each item.

Sample Answers:
2. a. Modern telecommunications could be useful in poorer countries. b. 4
3. a. There are a few recent developments that seem helpful. b. 4

8 Writing a Paragraph with Supporting Examples. Page 80.

Assign the exercise as homework after you go over the directions. Depending on the group, you may want to ask volunteers to suggest possible examples that would support each of the topic sentences. Go over the exercise, by having students share their paragraphs with partners.

Sample Answers:

1. Some days I feel that technology is my best friend. With e-mail and instant messages, I can talk with friends and family even though they are far away from me. I can browse the Internet and find newspapers in my own language. I can read a different perspective of the news. I can also use the computer to do my writing homework and the word-processing program helps correct my spelling and edit my work. Technology really helps me.

2. Some days I feel that technology is my worst enemy. The Internet is supposed to be quick and easy to use, but I can spend hours looking for some little piece of information. Then the computer crashes, and I have to start all over. Other times, I'm trying to print out something, and the printer jams or I run out of ink (toner). So my work is late all because of technology.

3. I think I am one of the luckiest people in the world. I have the opportunity to study and learn more. Others in my family have not been able to do this. I have some wonderful friends. We do a lot of things together and they help me with my English. Other people take education and friends for granted, but I realize how lucky I am to have them.

What Do You Think?

Using Cellular Phones

Arrange students in groups of four to talk about their own views and experiences related to cell phones. Give the groups about 15-20 minutes to discuss the questions. Circulate among the groups, listening, and giving assistance as need. When all groups are finished, ask volunteers from each group to share the most interesting information and ideas from their groups.

Answers will vary.

Part 2 Tracks to the Future

Before You Read

1 **Identifying the Pattern of Organization. Page 81.**
Preview the reading selection by following the instructions for the exercise. Discuss the answers to the questions about the problem and solution. Call attention to the three patterns of organization. Point out the similarities and differences in the patterns. Then have students skim the reading selection and decide on the organizational pattern used. Go over the answer. Have volunteers explain how they decided on the pattern

Answer: Pattern 3

2 **Scanning to Complete Common Phrases. Page 82.**
Explain the instructions. Point out that the answer to the sample item is in the synopsis statement under the title of the reading selection. Have students complete the exercise and compare their answers with partners. Review the answers and ask volunteers to use the words and phrases in their own sentences.

Answers: 2. charge 3. congestion
4. sprawl 5. fleet 6. assembly 7. Deco
8. irreversible 9. trend 10. suburbs

Read

Tracks to the Future. Page 82.
[on tape/CD]
Read together the introductory information and guiding questions. Remind students to look for the answers to the questions as they go through the reading. Then, play the tape or CD and have students follow along in their books. Pause as needed to ask comprehension questions and to point out key vocabulary. Replay and reread the selection.

After You Read

3 Adding Suffixes to Form Nouns and Adjectives. Page 84.

Have students complete the exercise, referring back to the reading selection as needed. Go over the answers with the class.

Answers: 2. comfortable 3. inventor
4. maintenance 5. alliance 6. disappearance
7. construction 8. development 9. suburban
10. ownership 11. expansion 12. revival

4 Paraphrasing Key Ideas. Page 85.

Read the explanation on paraphrasing. Point out that the questions will guide their paraphrasing. Have students compare their answers with partners before going over possible answers with the group.

Sample Answers:

Changes by vested interests. The oil, tire, and auto companies were the vested interests. They made money from making the changes in transportation. They bought 100 street car companies in 45 cities. They replaced all the street cars with their buses and made a lot of money doing it.

Unforeseen consequences. The government started building a system of roads and freeways. They wanted to connect the cities and the suburbs, but as a consequence, they encouraged people to drive more. This created more congestion, air pollution, and smog.

Talk It Over

Read aloud the questions clarifying vocabulary as needed. Then allow 15-20 minutes for small group discussion of the answers. Ask groups to report their ideas.

Answers will vary.

5 Doing a Street Interview. Page 86.

Go over the interview questions with the group. You may want to assign the topics to students.

Allow time for students to interview each other. Then arrange students in groups according to their interview topics and have them discuss the results of their surveys. Ask volunteers from each group to summarize their interview findings. Alternatively, you may want to have students prepare a written report on their findings.

Focus on Testing

Computerized Testing

Preview the article on computerized testing. If possible, have the class view a sample on a computer. Encourage students to share any experiences they have had taking computerized tests. Call attention to the list of tips. Then have students scan the instructions, to complete the exercise. Go over the answers with the whole class.

Answers: 2. tutorial 3. adaptive 4. gender
5. format 6. overview 7. confirmed
8. screen 9. timer

Video Activities: Internet Publishing

Before You Watch

Read the questions aloud and ask students to discuss their answers in small groups. Have students report to the class their answers.

Culture Note

Ask students if they are familiar with Stephen King and his work. Bring in samples of books and names of popular films based on his work.

Answers:
1. 1–b 2–c 3–a
2. Answers will vary.

Watch [on video]

Ask students to read the questions to prepare them for the video. Then play the video and have them answer the questions. Review the answers together.

Answers: 1. a, c 2. a, c 3. b 4. c 5. c

Watch Again [on video]

Point out the questions and explain that students need to watch carefully to find the answers. Replay the video and have students complete the exercise. Go over the answers with the whole class to summarize the information.

Answers: 1. $1 for each installment
2. b 3. b

After You Watch

Assign this for homework. Allow time for students to share their articles with partners or in small groups.

Answers will vary.

Money Matters

Goals

- **Skim for the general idea**
- **Scan for members of word families**
- **Use the context to explain business terms**
- **Read between the lines**
- **Identify the setting, characters, and conflict**
- **Get the meaning of words from context**
- **Predict events in a narrative**
- **Recall idioms and expressions**

Part 1 Executive Takes Chance on Pizza, Transforms Spain

Read together the **In This Chapter** note to present the chapter topic. Guide discussion of business success stories students know.

Before You Read

1 Skimming for the General Idea. Page 90.
Preview the reading selection. Point out the title and photo. Then have students skim to find the three factors that helped the man succeed. Students can compare their answers with partners. The go over the responses with the whole class.

Sample Answers: The three factors that helped the man were:

1. the need for convenience food (the untapped market of the Spanish people)

2. his background growing up as a immigrant (his desire to find ways to succeed)

3. his understanding of the Spanish mentality (his Cuban-American background)

2 Scanning for Members of Word Families. Page 90.
Go over the instructions, pointing out the example of members of a word family. Then ask students to complete the exercise individually. Go over the answers with the group.

Answers: 2. convenience 3. modernize 4. management 5. prospered 6. specialties 7. affordable 8. mentality 9. maturing

Read

Executive Takes Chance on Pizza, Transforms Spain. Page 91. [on tape/CD]
Read together the introductory paragraph which gives background information on job trends and introduces Leopoldo Fernandez Pujols. Then play the tape or CD as students follow along in their books. You may want to stop the recording periodically to check understanding and point out key vocabulary. Listen a second time as students read along.

After You Read

3 Using the Context to Explain Business Terms. Page 93.
Read the instructions and have students complete the exercise. Then discuss the answers with the whole class. Ask volunteers to explain how they arrived at their definitions.

Answers:
2. involving many countries
3. planned or expected sales for the future

4. places where products are sold
5. a number of businesses owned by the same person or people
6. explosion or rapid growth of something
7. not exploited or used yet
8. markets that are growing; places where business will grow

4 Small Group Discussion. Page 94.

In this activity, students review and analyze the success story of TelePizza and share their own insights about the story. Ask volunteers to report their groups' responses. Summarize the responses.

Sample Answers:

1. At first, Mr. Fernandez had problems keeping up with the growth management. He had trouble managing the money, the people, and with training people.
2. TelePizza is doing well because pizza is a popular food item and Mr. Fernandez probably has a very good personality for the business. He is dynamic and hardworking.
3. The Spanish nutritionist thinks the recent eating habits have changed for the worse. It is not as good as the traditional Mediterranean diet. I agree with her opinion.
4. Popular "fast foods" are tacos, pizza, hamburgers, fries. I like them once in a while, but not all the time.
5. Mr. Fernandez's Cuban-American background helps him because he knows the language and culture of the Spanish population so it makes it easier for him to start a business there.

Talk It Over

This activity allows students to consider the expansion plans of the TelePizza business. Arrange students in groups of four. Give the groups about 15-20 minutes to discuss the questions. Circulate among the groups, listening, and giving assistance as need. When all groups are finished, ask volunteers from each group to share their reactions to the expansion ideas.

Answers will vary.

Around the Globe

In this activity, students consider business advice of famous entrepreneurs from around the world. Ask students to share information they know about the various people. Have volunteers suggest what the entrepreneurs are saying in the quotes. Then have students work individually to write a paragraph about one of the quotes. When students are finished, have them share their responses with partners and give suggestions on their partners' work. Ask volunteers to share their readings with the whole class.

Answers will vary.

Focus on Testing

Reading Between the Lines

Read together the instructions. Call attention to the common incorrect choices used on inference tests. Then have students read the paragraphs and answer the questions. As you go over the answers with the class, ask volunteers to explain why the other choices are not correct.

Answers: 1. c 2. d 3. b

Part 2 The Luncheon

Before You Read

1 Identifying the Setting, Characters, and Conflict. Page 97.

Use the information in the notes to clarify the meanings of character, setting and plot. Then have students scan to find these narrative elements for The Luncheon on pages 99-103. Go over the answers together. Have volunteers point out information in the reading where they found or inferred the answers.

Sample Answers:
1. 20 years ago; Paris, France (in the Latin Quarter)
2. The woman is rich. She reads books. She's a pushy and talkative person. She's quite imposing in size and about 40 years old.
3. The conflict is that this woman has invited herself to lunch expecting that the man would pay for the luncheon. The man doesn't' have a lot of money, but doesn't want to be rude to the woman by saying no or by telling her about the problem.

After you read the note about conflict, climax, and resolution, guide students to make predications about what will happen.

2 Getting the Meaning of Words from Context. Page 97.

Go over the instructions. Students can work with partners to complete the exercise. Go over the answers and encourage volunteers to explain how they made their choices.

Answers: 2. a 3. b 4. a 5. c 6. a 7. c 8. b 9. b 10. c

Read

3 Predicting Events in a Narrative. Page 99.

Read together the preliminary information about William Somerset Maugham and the directions about making predictions. Point out examples of the questions in the story on pages 100-103. Read the selection as students follow along in their books. Have students make predictions by answering the italicized questions in the selection. At the end, ask volunteers to summarize the plot and give their reactions to the woman in the story. You may want to have the students listen as you read the story again. You may also want to have students read the story again silently for enjoyment.

After You Read

4 Recalling Idioms and Expressions. Page 103.

Have students complete the exercise, referring back to the reading selection as needed. Go over the answers with the class.

Answers: *caught sight of;* does fly; body and soul; beyond happiness; sank; took him quite seriously to task; caring now; taken a hand

Talk It Over

This activity gives students a chance to voice their thoughts and reactions to the characters and conflict in the story. Arrange students in groups of four or five to talk about their own ideas about the story and situation. Allow 15-20 minutes for discussion. Allow time for groups to report their ideas.

Sample Answers:
1. The woman was very self-centered and did not think about other people. She is spoiled and no one has ever told her no to anything. I think she took advantage of the young man. She never asked. She just

demanded and made it awkward to refuse her requests.

2. The young man should have chosen a restaurant he preferred. He might have faked an appointment and cut short the luncheon. He was trapped by the rules of courtesy and good manners. Under the circumstances, I would have cut the luncheon short.

3. The irony was that the woman only ate "one thing at lunch" and yet at the end of the story, she was quite fat.

4. Answers will vary.

5. Some people refuse to live within their income level. They want more or they want to give the impression that they are well-off. Credit cards make it easy for people to live beyond their means. I don't think that it's lack of experience or training. I think it is more the society has made it seem that we constantly need to be consuming and buying more and more things and living at a certain level.

6. The best rule for managing money is not to buy more than you can pay for right now.

What Do You Think?

Buying on the Internet.

Read together Buying on the Internet. Then have students discuss their Internet shopping experiences or experiences of friends or acquaintances by answering the questions. After 10-15 minutes of small group discussion, have volunteers report to the class the most interesting points of their discussions.

Answers will vary.

Video Activities: Welfare Payments

Before You Watch

Read the questions aloud and have students discuss their answers in small groups. Have students report to the class their answers.

Sample Answers: 1. a, b 2. c 3. Graft is a crime where a person uses their position or power to get money or some advantage.

Watch [on video]

Ask students to read the questions to prepare them for the video. Then play the video and have them answer the questions. Review the answers together.

Answers: 1. b 2. a 3. a 4. c 5. b

Watch Again [on video]

Point out the questions and explain that students need to watch carefully to find the answers. Replay the video and have students complete the exercise. Go over the answers with the whole class to summarize the information.

Answers: 1. 70 2. 60 3. 20 4. 20-30

After You Watch

Assign this for homework. Allow time for students to share their articles and word family members with partners or in small groups.

Answers will vary.

Remarkable Individuals

Goals

- Skim for the general idea
- Figure out words from structure clues
- Identify key terms
- Form related words
- Infer meaning
- Support general statements
- Use a title and illustrations to predict
- Identify positive and negative points
- Make a comparison and contrast
- Preview for organization
- Use expressive synonyms
- Identify the voices in a reading
- Preview test questions
- Use noun suffixes

Part 1 Confucius, 551 B.C.E.-479 B.C.E.

Introduce the topic of remarkable people by reading together the **In This Chapter** note on page 107. Allow volunteers to share names of people they think are or were remarkable.

Before You Read

1 **Skimming for the General Idea. Page 108.**
Read together the directions. Have students refer back to page 40 for information on skimming. After students complete the exercise, go over the answer. Ask volunteers to explain why the other choices are not good general idea statements.

Encourage volunteers to share other information they may know about Confucius.

Answer: c

2 **Figuring Out Words from Structure Clues. Page 108.**
Go over the instructions together. Modeling how to break up the word "childhood" into parts. Point out the explanation and sample answer for the word. Model other words as needed. Then have students complete the exercise individually or in pairs. Go over the answers with the class.

Answers: 2. information about someone's past experiences 3. territory that is governed by a prince 4. main points or underlying ideas and principles 5. wanting to do good for others 6. thoughts about things in the future or future expectations 7. a person who defends or protects 8. a person who makes new things 9. are common or normal.

Read

Confucius, 551 B.C.E. – 479 B.C.E. Page 109. [on tape/CD]
Play the tape or CD as students follow along in their books. You may want to stop the recording from time to time to check understanding and point out vocabulary words. Listen a second time as students read along.

After You Read

3 **Identifying Key Terms. Page 110.**
Have students complete the exercise. Then discuss the answers with the whole class.

Answers: 2. g 3. d 4. b 5. f 6. e

4 **Forming Related Words. Page 111.**
As you read aloud the explanation, ask volunteers to suggest adjective, adverb, and verb endings. For

example: adjective endings: *-ing, -ed, -al, -an;* adverb ending: *-ly;* verb endings: *-ize, -ate, -fy.* Then have students complete the exercise. Students can check back in the reading for the words. Go over the answers together.

Answers: 2. influential 3. easily 4. political 5. primarily 6. governmental 7. Confucian 8. philosophical 9. modernize

5 Inferring Meaning. Page 111.

Have students complete the exercise. Go over the answers. Ask volunteers to use the words in sentences.

Answers: 2. e 3. n 4. h 5. b 6. l 7. k 8. o 9. c 10. f 11. m 12. a 13. g 14. i 15. d

6 Supporting General Statements. Page 111.

Read together the instructions. Students can work with partners or in small groups to find facts from the reading to support the statements. Ask volunteers to share their answers with the class.

Sample Answers:
1. He was born in a small principality. He was reared in poverty and had no formal education.
2. The state exists for the benefit of the people, not the rulers. A leader should govern primarily by moral example, rather than by force.
3. Shih Huang Ti...decided to reform the country entirely and make a complete break with the past. He ordered the burning of all copies of Confucius' works. Most Confucian books were indeed destroyed...
4. The civil service examinations in China were based primarily on knowledge of Confucian classics. Since those examinations were the main route by which commoners could enter the administration and achieve political power, the governing class... was composed of men who had carefully

studied the works of Confucius and absorbed his principles.

The Communist party seized power. It was their belief that, in order both to modernize China and to eliminate economic injustice, it was necessary to make radical changes in society. As the ideas of Confucius were highly conservative, the communists made a major effort to eradicate his influence.

Talk It Over

In this activity, students share their opinions and views on Confucianism and governments. Arrange students in groups of four. Give the groups about 15-20 minutes to discuss the questions. Circulate among the groups, listening, and giving assistance as need. When all groups are finished, ask volunteers from each group to share the most interesting information and ideas from their groups.

Answers will vary.

Around the Globe

This activity allows students to compare and contrast two contemporary leaders and their influence on their countries. Students work with partners or in small groups reading about the leaders and then answering the questions that follow. Circulate as students work, d giving assistance as needed. Ask volunteers to share their answers with the class. Discuss other information students may know about these leaders.

Sample Answers:
1. Vicente Fox has won attention for his efforts for the fair treatment of Mexico's Indian population and for his national micro-lending problem to improve the life of everyone in the country.
2. Kim Dae-jung has achieved recognition for his work towards peace and reconciliation with North Korea. He wants to end the division and hostility which has existed between North and South Korea.
3. & 4. Answers will vary.

Making Connections

Allow time for students to research the lives and work of one of the three people covered in Part 1. Ask volunteers to present their findings to the class.

Part 2 Beating the Odds

Before You Read

1 **Using a Title and Illustrations to Predict. Page 114.**

As you read aloud the directions, clarify the gambling reference in the title. Then tell students to skim the article to get a general idea of the life and character of Oprah Winfrey. After students complete the exercise, go over the answers together.

Sample Answers:
The title tells us that Oprah Winfrey didn't have a good chance at succeeding in life. There were many factors against here success. She probably had to struggle and work hard for what she achieved.

By looking at the photographs, she seems like a very proud and happy person. She looks wealthy and self-confident. She is poised and seems secure about herself.

2 **Using Context and Structure to Get Meaning. Page 114.**

Read together the instructions. Review as needed different types of context clues and sentence structures that can be used to help guess the meanings of unfamiliar words. Have students complete the exercise. Then go over the answers together. Ask volunteers to explain how they decided on the meanings.

Answers: 2. b 3. b 4. a 5.d 6. c 7. b
8. b 9. a 10. d

Read

Beating the Odds. Page 116.

Read together the background information about Oprah Winfrey and Africa -American history. Clarify as needed. Then have students read along in their books as you read the selection. You may want to pause from time to time to ask comprehension questions and point out key vocabulary. Ask volunteers to summarize the information.

After You Read

3 **Identifying Positive and Negative Points. Page 118.**

Have pairs complete the exercise, referring back to the reading selection as needed. Then ask students to compare their lists in small groups. Guide students to summarize the positive and negative influences mentioned in the reading.

Sample Answers:
Positive Influences: grandmother (attention), church, school, Vernon Winfrey and his family (discipline), Upward Bound program, scholarship to middle-class school, return to her father's family

Negative Influences: poverty, racial climate of the time, single mother, prejudice, her move to Milwaukee with little supervision or attention, summer with her mother in the "boarding house" atmosphere, sexual abuse, turmoil at home, alienation at school, running away

4 **Recalling Vocabulary. Page 118.**

Ask students to complete the vocabulary exercise individually. Students can compare their answers with partners. As you go over the answers with the class, ask volunteers to use the vocabulary words in their own sentences.

Answers: 2. poverty 3. tumultuous
4. hospitable 5. exceedingly 6. affluent
7. poise 8. ambiguous 9. alienation
10. rebellious 11. turmoil 12. on the lam

Talk It Over

Before arranging students in small groups for discussion, read aloud the questions and clarify new vocabulary as needed. Then allow 15-20 minutes for discussion. Ask volunteers from each group to report their ideas.

Answers will vary.

5 Making a Comparison and Contrast. Page 119.

Go over the instructions for the activity. You may want to have volunteers suggest some similarities and differences between Confucius and Oprah Winfrey to demonstrate making comparisons and contrasts. Students may want to share their outlines with partners before writing the essay. Invite volunteers to share their essays with the class.

Answers will vary.

Part 3 Courage Begins with One Voice

Before You Read

1 Previewing for Organization. Page 120.

As you read together the instructions, clarify vocabulary, such as: *human rights* and *oppressed*. Call attention to the three patterns of organization commonly used in articles. Then ask students to skim the essay to determine which pattern is used. Have volunteers explain the reasons for their choice as you go over the answer.

Answer: 2

2 Using Expressive Synonyms. Page 120.

After you go over the instructions, have students complete the exercise individually. Have students compare their answers with partners. Then, go over the answers with the whole class.

Answers: 2. eloquence 3. valor
4. overwhelming 5. take up the torch
6. atrocities 7. compelling 8. sacrifice
9. monitors 10. obstacles 11. conduct
12. atone

Read

Courage Begins with One Voice. Page 120.

Play the tape or CD as students read along in their books. You may want to pause at the end of each section to point out key vocabulary and have volunteers summarize the information. Replay the recording and have students reread the selection.

After You Read

3 Identifying the Voices in a Reading. Page 124.

Go over the instructions. Then have students try to match the quotes with the correct speakers based on what they remember. Students can compare their answers with partners and check back in the essay if they don't agree. Go over the answers with the class. Have volunteers point out the clues that they used to find the answers.

Answers: 1. D 2. A 3. B 4. E 5. C

Focus on Testing

Previewing the Questions

Read together the test-taking tips about previewing questions. Then have students time themselves as they complete the quiz. After students check their answers with partners, go over the responses. Have volunteers point out and correct the information in the false statements.

Answers: 1. F 2. T 3. F 4. F 5. T 6. F
7. F 8. T 9. F 10. F 11. T 12. F

1. The author spent two years interviewing
   51 people from 40 countries.

3. Bonded labor is a system by which a
   poor child is taken care of by a host
   family and forced to work like a slave.

4. Kailash Satyarthi of India continues to
   work to free child workers after two of her
   colleagues were killed.

6. Havel believes that a true leader like the
   Dalai Lama stands up for the opinions
   against the majority.

7. Kek Galabru helped negotiate an end to
   the Cambodian Civil War in 1991.

9. Oscar Arias Sanchez, a former president
   of Costa Rica, was awarded the Nobel
   Peace Prize in 1987.

10. Arias Sanchez believes that the way to
    end conflict in Central America is to
    support democracy and to demilitarize
    the world.

12. Juliana Dogbadzi escaped from the
    Trokosi system and now travels in Ghana
    speaking against this practice.

4 Using Noun Suffixes. Page 126.

Review the suffixes used to change verbs and
adjectives to nouns. Then have students complete
the exercise. Go over the answers with the class.
Have volunteers suggest other sentences for the
nouns.

Answers: 2. expression 3. commitment
4. repression 5. responsibility 6. assistance
7. negotiations 8. preparation
9. demilitarization 10. investments
11. decisions 12. servitude

What Do You Think?

This can be done as a whole class or a small group
activity. Try to find several examples of good and
bad leaders that everyone agrees on. Then guide

discussion of the questions. You may want to have
students write up their own thoughts on
characteristics and examples in an essay.

Answers will vary.

Video Activities: Overcoming Serious Illness

Before You Watch

Read the questions aloud and ask students to
discuss their answers in small groups. Have
students report to the class their answers.

Sample Answers: 1. a 2. b

Watch [on video]

Ask students to read the questions to prepare
them for the video. Then play the video and have
them answer the questions. Review the answers
together.

Answers: 1. b 2. c 3. a, c 4. a 5. c
6. determined, courageous, hardworking

Watch Again [on video]

Point out the questions and explain that students
need to watch carefully to find the answers.
Replay the video and have students complete the
exercise. Go over the answers with the whole
class to summarize the information.

Answers: 1. a 2. "Start slow and better."
3. c

After You Watch

Assign this research activity for homework. Have
students share the information they find with the
rest of the class.

Answers will vary.

Creativity

Part 1 Guggenheim Museum U.S.A.

Introduce the chapter topic by reading together the **In This Chapter** note on page 129. Guide discussion of people that students consider as being creative. Talk about different media for creative people.

Before You Read

1   **Vocabulary of Shapes and Forms. Page 130.**
Read together the information and call attention to the drawings and labels. Then have students complete the exercise. Go over the answers with the class. Encourage volunteers to identify other shapes and forms that they know.

Answers: 1. cube 2. triangle 3. rectangle 4. polygon 5. cone 6. spiral, helix

2   **Small Group Discussion. Page 130.**
Before arranging students in small groups for discussion, read aloud the questions and clarify vocabulary as needed. After 10-15 minutes of discussion, have volunteers report to the class the most interesting information and ideas from their groups.

Sample Answers:
1.   Answers will vary.
2.   Some outstanding buildings in other cities are: the Taj Mahal (India), Angkor Wat (Cambodia), Versailles (France), the Vatican (Italy), the Hermitage (Russia), etc.
3.   These buildings are remarkable because of the history associated with the places, the style of architecture and decoration of the buildings, the lines and style, etc.
4.   Answers will vary.

Read

Guggenheim Museum U.S.A. Page 131.
Use the introductory paragraph to guide students as they preview the reading selection. Tell students to think about the question to guide them as complete the reading assignment. Read the selection as students follow along in their books. You may want to stop occasionally to ask comprehension questions and point out important vocabulary words. Have students listen as you read a second time.

After You Read

3   **Making Inferences and Drawing Conclusions. Page 134.**
Review making inferences and drawing conclusions as needed. Call attention to the sample in item #1. Then have students work with partners or in small groups to make their own inferences and conclusions about Frank Lloyd

Wright. Discuss the responses with the whole class. Have volunteers support their inferences and conclusions.

Sample Answers:

2. Wright had many assistants to attend to all the details of the work. Many people wanted to work with Wright. The assistants admired Wright and his work. They stayed with him for a long time.

3. Wright was not concerned if there were minor structural problems. He was more concerned with the large ideas and concepts of the buildings. He thought he was always right and others should not question the end results. The owners didn't have to understand and appreciate everything about his buildings.

4 Use Context Clues. Page 134.

Have students complete the vocabulary exercise. Then go over the answers with the group.

Answers: 2. pioneer 3. obstinacy
4. conventional 5. fatigue, weariness 6. smirk

Talk It Over

This activity allows students to discuss their thoughts and ideas about Frank Lloyd Wright, the Guggenheim Museum, and architecture. Arrange students in groups of four. Give the groups about 15-20 minutes to discuss the questions. Circulate among the groups, listening, and giving assistance as need. When all groups are finished, ask volunteers from each group to share the most interesting information and ideas from their groups.

Sample Answers:

1. Wright's design was innovative because is had a circular interior. The building spirals downward. He chose this way to make it easier for museum goers to walk through and enjoy the exhibits at the same angle that the artists created them.

2. I think this is an opinion. There is nothing to support it as a fact that people don't

go there to see the art work. It is a view on how people feel and think about the museum.

3 - 5. Answers will vary.

Focus on Testing

Thinking Twice About Tricky Questions

This section helps students develop strategies for taking multiple-choice questions. Read together the information, calling attention to the sample test questions. Have students read through the test items and decide which are memory questions and which ones are inference questions. Have students complete the exercise. Students can check their answers with partners. Go over any questions that were difficult for the group.

Answers: 1. a 2. b 3. c 4. c 5. a 6. b

Part 2 If You Invent the Story, You're the First to See How It Ends

Before You Read

1 Getting the Meaning of Words in Context. Page 137.

Read aloud the directions and go over the example together. If needed, review using context clues to guess meanings. After students complete the exercise, go over the answers together.

Answers: 2. c 3. b 4. d 5. a 6. a 7. c 8. b 9. c 10. c

2 Finding the Basis for Inferences. Page 138.

Clarify the instructions. Call attention to the sample item. Point out the information in the line from the story that supports the inference about the author living in the country. You may want to have volunteers suggest possible information that would support the other inferences before asking students to scan the reading for supporting lines. Students can compare their answers. Go over the responses with the whole group.

Answers:

2. ...He kept turning and talking to the woman... He seemed friendly and affectionate.

3. ... She never turned to look at him or answer... She sat without movement or response, staring straight ahead.

4. I supposed... I wondered... Perhaps he was... Perhaps... Or maybe...

5. I write about the things that disturb me, the things that won't let me alone, the things that are eating slowly at my brain at 3 in the morning, the things that unbalance my world.

3 Small Group Discussion. Page 139.

Use the questions to promote discussion of authors and the creative writing process. Invite volunteers to share some of the ideas and information from their groups' discussions with the whole class.

Answers will vary.

Read

If You Invent the Story, You're the First to See How it Ends. Page 139.

You may want to have students make predictions about the content of the article based on the inferences in Exercise 2 and the discussions from Exercise 3. Have students read along in their books as you read the selection. Pause as needed to check comprehension and discuss vocabulary and expressions. Encourage students to give their responses to the article. Then ask students to follow along as you read the selection again.

After You Read

4 Building Suspense. Page 140.

Clarify the meaning of *suspense* and *mystery* as you read together the instructions for the exercise. Have students complete the exercise, referring back to the reading selection as needed. Go over the answers with the class.

Sample Answers:

2. wife; trying to win her back after a fight

3. daughter; trying to comfort her about some problem

4. his dog

5. The process of writing is unpredictable and humbling. Writing is trying to work something out for yourself. It is a very private matter.

5 Identifying Synonyms from Parallel Constructions. Page 141.

Explain parallel construction and point out the example of it in the first item. Go over the instructions. Remind students to use the clues in the sentences to guess the meanings of the italicized words. Students can compare their answers with partners before you go over possible responses.

Sample Answers:

2. Arrogant; *Imperious* means acting like an emperor who doesn't care or isn't concerned about others.

3. stony-faced; *Implacable* means not moving or not able to be moved like a stone without any feelings or responses.

4. tender; *Dedicated* means in a gentle and concerned way.

5. paralyzed; *Miserable* means very uncomfortable or painful.

6. trouble; *Disturb* means to bother, annoy, or interrupt.

6 Writing Your Own Group Mystery. Page 142.

Read together the instructions, pointing out that students will be creating an original mystery story.

Call attention to the three parts needed for the story. Go over the possible story ideas. Then arrange students in groups of 4-5 to plan their own chain story. Go around the room, listening and giving assistance as needed. Ask volunteers from each group to share their story with the class.

Answers will vary.

Talk It Over

Arrange students in groups of four or five to talk about their own thoughts on mystery, suspense, and writers. Allow 15-20 minutes for discussion. Allow time for groups to report their ideas.

Sample Answers:

1. Some horror films are *Psycho, The Haunting, The Exorcist.* They are scary because you don't know what is going to happen, but you know it's going to be something terrible. They often build suspense with music, with making the viewer expect something bad to happen. The films give you clues, but it's unclear who or what is dangerous.

2. Some people write to make something beautiful. Others write for themselves. Others write to tell their feelings and thoughts to others. Some write to teach others. Some write to make people laugh. The writer of this selection writes to make sense of the world to herself.

3. I think that it is difficult to be a writer. You want to express your ideas very clearly, to make the language correct and meaningful to others. Some advantages of being a writer is that you don't need a lot of equipment or a big office. You can work by yourself. You can work at your own pace. Some disadvantages are that you might not make a lot of money by writing. It probably is hard to get started so people know your work.

4 & 5. Answers will vary.

Part 3 We Can't Just Sit Back and Hope

Before You Read

1   **Previewing for Point of View. Page 142.**
Read together the explanation and notes on point of view. Then ask students to skim the interview and decide on the best description of Steven Spielberg. Go over the answer. Ask them to point out information that supports their choice.

Answer: 2

Read

We Can't Just Sit Back and Hope. Page 143. [on tape/CD]

Read together the introductory paragraph. Ask students to name films they know by director Steven Spielberg. Tell students to think about the director as a person and his motivation for making films. Play the tape or CD as students follow along in their books. Pause occasionally to ask comprehension questions and point out important vocabulary words. Listen a second time as students read along. Ask them to describe Steven Spielberg and tell what motivates him.

After You Read

2   **Finding Synonyms. Page 145.**
Have students complete the exercise individually. Go over the answers.

Answers: 2. obsession 3. unique
4. recurring 5. academic 6. old-fashioned
7. censor

3   **Paraphrasing Main Ideas. Page 145.**
Students can work in small groups to explain the main ideas expressed in the interview. As you go

over the answers with the class, ask volunteers to point out details that support the main ideas.

Sample Answers:

1. Spielberg was the oldest child with three younger sisters, so he was always looking for ways to get special attention. Since he was a good storyteller, he began using a movie camera to tell his stories.

2. His parents' divorce was probably a painful experience for him and he has included divorce as a theme in some of his movies.

3. Spielberg doesn't believe in censorship. He does think that people who make movies should be responsible for the content.

4. Spielberg always has been hopeful. He thinks that people need to act and voice opinions. They should do something to fix the world.

5. Spielberg is a creative person who loves to tell stories. He has old-fashioned views and he's a caring, concerned, and responsible person and film director.

Making Connections

Assign the projects for individual or group work. Students may want to be present their findings in written form or in an oral presentation.

Answers will vary.

Talk It Over

Encourage students to express their thoughts and opinions on family position, luck, values, censorship, and movies as art. Students can use information from the reading selection or their own experiences to support their answers. Arrange students in groups of four or five. After

15 minutes of discussion, have volunteers report to the class the most interesting ideas from their discussions.

Sample Answers:

1. I think that the oldest child is usually more serious and studious than the others because he or she often has to take care of the younger brothers and sisters. The youngest child is often more spoiled and likes to play more. The youngest usually doesn't have the same chores and responsibilities in the family as the older children.

2. In my opinion, luck played a role in Spielberg's becoming a director. His first film was noticed by the right people.

3. Old-fashioned values are love, family, good over evil. I think these values make more optimistic films that make people feel better about themselves and what they can do.

4. I think there should be more censorship of films. Films are getting to graphic. It makes people feel that killing and extra-marital sex are normal and good for people.

5. Answers will vary.

What Do You Think?

Creativity in Men and Women

You may want to read together this section before arranging students in groups for discussion. As students work in small groups, go around giving assistance as needed. After 10-15 minutes of discussion, have volunteers report to the class the most interesting points of their discussions.

Answers will vary.

Video Activities: A Life of Painting

Before You Watch

Read the questions aloud and ask students to discuss their answers in small groups. Have students report to the class their answers.

Sample Answers: 1. 65 2. Yes. They usually really enjoy their work. The work defines their lives or gives meaning to their lives.

Watch [on video]

Ask students to read the questions to prepare them for the video. Then play the video and have them answer the questions. Review the answers together.

Answers: 1. painter 2. painter 3. a, d 4. The Big Apple 5. shock 6. their jobs 7. c, d, e

Watch Again [on video]

Point out the questions and explain that students need to watch carefully to find the answers. Replay the video and have students complete the exercise. Go over the answers with the whole class to summarize the information.

Answers:
1. *New Yorkers milling on Broadway* and *A whimsical moon city*
2. No _Sun_ Without _Shadow_
3. 1- more than 70 years, 2- 60 years, 3- 1966, 4- seven, 5- 96 years old
4. I'm as _excited_ now when I _start a painting_ as I was _70 years ago_.

After You Watch

Assign this for homework. Review synonyms, antonyms, and related words as needed. Allow time for students to share their lists of words.

Answers will vary.

Human Behavior

Goals
- Skim for the main idea
- Scan for the development of the main idea
- Get the meaning of words from context
- Find support for main ideas
- Find statements and implied ideas in passages
- Preview for characters and plot
- Make inferences about characters
- Express the theme
- Preview for rhyme and rhythm
- Paraphrase figurative language

Part 1 Ethnocentrism

Read together the **In This Chapter** note on page 149. Ask volunteers to share information they know about the work of anthropologists, psychologists, and sociologists. You may want to make a list of vocabulary and students' ideas and views for reference as you go through the chapter on human behavior.

Before You Read

1 **Skimming for the Main Idea. Page 150.**
Read about "ethnocentrism." Then tell students to skim to find the meaning of it. Go over the answer. Have volunteers point out where they found the author's explanation of it in the first two paragraphs.

Answer: Ethnocentrism is the belief that your own culture is better than any other.

2 **Scanning for the Development of the Main Idea. Page 150.**
Ask students to scan the article for the answers to the questions.

Answers: 1. 5 paragraphs 2. food preferences, language, myths and folktales

3 **Small Group Discussion. Page 150.**
Allow students to share their background knowledge about anthropologists and anthropology. Have volunteers share the groups' ideas and answers to the questions.

Sample Answers:
1. I imagine that anthropologists are old people who live with exotic tribal groups. They wear khaki clothes and write lots of notes. They learn the language of the tribe and live as the people they study do.
2. Answers will vary.
3. I think people who study anthropology enjoy learning about strange cultures and customs. They like to see what types of customs are universal and which ones are unique to different groups.

Read

Ethnocentrism. Page 150.
Go over the introductory paragraph before the article. Check the dictionary definition of *anthropology* with students' definitions. Read the selection as students follow along in their books. You may want to stop from time to time to check understanding and point out key vocabulary. Have students listen a second time as you read the selection.

After You Read

4   Scanning for Words. Page 153.

Read the instructions and go over the example. Have students complete the exercise. Then discuss the answers with the whole class.

Answers: 2. liberal; open-minded 3. bias
4. self-evaluation 5. repulsive; repugnant
6. barbarian 7. hue 8. inconceivable

5   Finding Support for Main Ideas. Page 153.

Depending on the group, you may want to have students work with partners to find examples from the selection to support the main ideas. Students can do the exercise orally or in writing. Then go over the answers with the group.

Answers:

1. Ethnocentrism is present in language. The Aleutian Indians used the word "eskimo" to refer to the people who live in the arctic and subarctic regions and eat food different from the food the Aleutian Indians ate. "Eskimo" means "eaters of raw flesh." The people of the arctic and subarctic regions called themselves "Inuit." The word "Inuit" means "real people." So, they consider themselves normal and others as different, not normal. Also the word "barbarian" was used by the Greeks to refer to tribes of people who spoke different languages. The Greeks thought the languages sounded like dogs barking, so "bar-bar" was the Greek word for the sound of the dog. The people who didn't speak Greek were "barbarian" or sounding like dogs barking.

2. Ethnocentrism is present in myths. In the Cherokee creation myth, the Creator made different clay figures. The white figure was not done enough. The black one was burnt and no good. But the red-brown figure was just right. So the Cherokees considered themselves to be normal and people of other races to be inferior.

3. Ethnocentrism is present in food preferences. In southeast Asia, people don't drink milk, but Americans think milk is a normal food. Dog meat is served in China, but most Americans would not consider eating dog meat. Horse meat is popular in some places, but Americans would not eat horse meat.

Talk It Over

Allow students in small groups to discuss their ideas and thoughts on culture shock and ethnocentrism. After 15-20 minutes of discussion, ask volunteers to share with the class the groups' responses and any interesting information.

Sample Answers:

1. Culture shock is the surprise and clash of values that comes from being in or encountering a different culture from one's own. It occurs when you observe or experience life in a culture different from your own. It can be a good or bad experience. If the person approaches the new culture with an open-mind, he or she can begin to see the reasons why the other culture has different customs or traditions. It can be bad, though, if the person does not respect the ways of the other culture or tries to change it without understanding it first.

2. Another example might be the American belief that democracy is the best form of government and American attempts to push other countries to adopt it. Some Americans also think that English should be the only language spoken in the United States.

3. I think the purpose of the article is to explain the meaning of it and to give some general examples. It's an introduction to ethnocentrism which will probably be followed by some articles or studies of some specific cultural groups or human culture.

4. If I were asked to eat dog or snake meat, I would be polite and take some. Obviously if the people of that culture eat it, it can't be bad. I would only refuse if there were some ethical, religious, or dietary reasons which prevented eating those items.

5. Answers will vary.

Focus on Testing

Finding Statements and Implied Ideas in Passages

Read together the explanation, clarifying *implied* and *directly stated* as needed. Then have students read the instructions and complete the exercise. Remind them to choose the correct answer and to note the line number where the answer was found. Go over the answers with the whole class.

Answers: 1. c; line 5 2. d; line 7 3. d; line 12 4. b; line 33 5. b; lines 54-55 6. c; lines 68-69

Part 2 A Clean, Well-Lighted Place

Before You Read

1 Previewing for Characters and Plot. Page 156.

Read aloud the background information on Ernest Hemingway and his style of writing. Ask students to skim the story to find the answers to the questions. Point out that students will need to make inferences to determine some of the answers. After students complete the exercise, go over the answers together.

Sample Answers: 1. There are three characters in the story. 2. The dialogue seems

to predominate. There is more dialogue than action. 3. The general tone of the story is sad. It's night. The characters seem to be either lonely or unhappy with what they are doing.

2 Getting the Meaning of Words from Context. Page 156.

Call attention to the italicized word in each of the exercise items. Tell students to read the excerpts and use context clues to guess the meanings of the italicized words. Go over the answers, having volunteers explain how they made their choices.

Answers: 2. c 3. a 4. b 5. a 6. c

Read

A Clean, Well-Lighted Place. Page 158.

Have students work individually reading the story. Alternatively, you may want to have students read the story with partners or in small groups. Encourage students to use context clues to help get the meaning of unfamiliar words. Ask volunteers to describe the characters and the setting and to summarize the story.

After You Read

3 Making Inferences About Characters. Page 162.

Go over the instructions, reviewing making inferences as needed. Call attention to the words that are often used to express inferences. Use the sample to clarify the instructions for the exercise. Have students complete the exercise. As you go over the answers with the class, ask volunteers to explain how they arrived at their inferences.

Sample Answers:
2. The waiter must think that people with money have nothing to worry about. Perhaps some people think that rich people don't have problems.

3. The younger waiter probably wants to go home. Maybe he doesn't care at all about others, especially this old man. Perhaps

he wishes that the old man were dead so the waiter wouldn't have to stay at work any longer.

4. The older waiter must be sympathetic with the old man's situation. Maybe the older waiter enjoys sitting alone in cafés in the evening. Perhaps he understands the old man better than the young waiter.

5. The older waiter must be thinking about the "nothing" reason for the man's failed attempt at suicide. Perhaps the older waiter also is sad about "nothing."

4 Expressing the Theme. Page 163.

Read the explanation of theme. Call attention to the three statements of theme for the story. Encourage students to consider which they like the best and explain why it is the best. Have volunteers give their choices and supporting reasons.

Answers will vary.

Talk It Over

Arrange students in groups of four or five to talk about their own thoughts on the characters and writer's craft. Set aside 15-20 minutes for discussion. Allow time for groups to report their ideas.

Sample Answers:
1. I think the waiter meant that there are two types of people: those who care about others and those who are self-centered and unconcerned about others. It's a generalization that is quite sharp, and I think in general it is true. But there are also many people that are somewhere in between the two extremes.

2. I think Hemingway used some Spanish words in the story to give it atmosphere. Also the use of "nada" in the prayer makes the "nothing" stand out even more than if Hemingway had used the English word "nothing."

3. I think the most important element in the story is the characters. It is through their dialog that you learn about the whole situation and the loneliness of the characters. It is the sharp contrast between the younger and older waiters that is so important for the theme.

Part 3 The Spell of the Yukon

1 Previewing for Rhyme and Rhythm. Page 164.

Use the explanation of rhyme and rhythm to review these poetic features. Have students listen for these features as you read aloud some of the poem. Then ask students to answer the questions. Go over the answers. Reread the portion of the poem for students to listen again for the features.

Answers:
1. Every other line rhymes in most cases. The pattern is a-b-a-b.

2. There are strong beats in each line. Usually there are 3 strong beat in each line.

2 Getting the Meaning of Words in Context. Page 164.

Discuss the information about Robert Service and his colorful style of writing as you read together the explanation and instructions. Then have students use the context clues to guess the meanings of some new words. Go over the answers, asking volunteers to point out the clues they used.

Answers: 1. b 2. c 3. d 4. c 5. d 6. a 7. d

Read together the background information about the poem and Robert Service's life and experiences in the Yukon. Have students consider the type of people that might have gone to the Yukon looking for gold.

Read

The Spell of the Yukon. Page 166. [on tape/CD]

Have students read along in their books as you play the tape or CD. You may want to have students listen once without reading. Then ask students to read the poem silently to themselves. Ask volunteers to describe the main character in the poem and how his feelings changed as he lived and worked in the Yukon.

After You Read

3 Small Group Discussion. Page 168.

This activity gives students a chance to express their own reactions and feelings about the poem. Arrange students in groups of four or five to talk about the answers to the questions. Allow 15-20 minutes for discussion. Ask groups to report their ideas.

Sample Answers:
1. A goldminer is supposed to be speaking in the poem. He is a rough, tough person. He's hardworking and loves the outdoors. His language is crude and non-standard, so he probably is not well-educated.
2. "Last fall" he found gold—a lot of gold. Right now, he's spending his money in wasteful ways. He may be losing it to gamblers. "They" probably refers to gamblers and people that want him to buy things.
3. He describes the Yukon as a beautiful place. It's rough but awe-inspiring. It's pristine. Each season has something beautiful and wonderful to the miner. I think I would like to see it, but I wouldn't like to live there all year long.
4. He thought he would be very happy to get the gold and the gold would make him happy. The gold isn't making him happy. It's not important. He liked the hard work and the beautiful land around

him. They have become more important to him.
5. The man plans to return back into the wilderness to live and work. I think he will make a cabin and continue living in the rugged country.

4 Paraphrasing Figurative Language. Page 168.

Explain figurative language and point out examples from the poem as needed. Call attention to the example with its explanation of the figurative language. Then have students give their own interpretations from the lines in the exercise. Students can compare their answers with others before you go over possible interpretations with the class.

Sample Answers:
1. I worked very hard during my youth. I worked too hard!
2. The land has a strong hold on you, like some bad habits. You start off being an enemy to the land, but you end up loving it or being its friend.
3. There is a lot of unexplored land and places. People haven't followed or mapped the rivers and land.
4. It is a dangerous place because there are so many times when you can barely survive.
5. I don't want the gold, but I like being there and looking for the gold.

Talk It Over

Students express their own opinions and feelings related to poet and his ideas about the wilderness. Arrange students in groups of four or five discuss their answers to the questions. Allow 15-20 minutes for discussion. Ask volunteers to report their groups' ideas.

Sample Answers:
1. Yes, I think many people feel disappointed when they finally reach a goal. The goal

was always pushing them on and when they get there, there is nothing more to do and they realize that they liked the hard work of striving for the goal.

2 - 5. Answers will vary

What Do You Think?

Blaming Others

You may want to read together this section before arranging students in groups for discussion. As students work in small groups, go around giving assistance as needed. After 10-15 minutes of discussion, have volunteers report to the class the most interesting points of their discussions.

Answers will vary.

Video Activities: People Skills

Before You Watch

Read the questions aloud and ask students to discuss their answers in small groups. Have students report to the class their answers.

Answers: 1. Answers will vary. 2. a, c

Watch [on video]

Ask students to read the questions to prepare them for the video. Then play the video and have them answer the questions. Review the answers together.

Answers: 1. c 2. a-3; b-1; c-2 3. c
4. The Jenkins project will be on hold until Debbie's pager comes on.

Watch Again [on video]

Point out the questions and explain that students need to watch carefully to find the answers. Replay the video and have students complete the exercise. Go over the answers with the whole class to summarize the information.

Answers: 1. B 2. A 3. Charles, Maria, Edward 4. c

After You Watch

Assign this for homework. Allow time for students to share their character descriptions with the others in the class.

Answers will vary.

Crime and Punishment

Goals
- **Get meaning from context**
- **Skim for organization in biography**
- **Find examples to support main ideas**
- **Scan for compound-word synonyms**
- **Identify narrative elements**
- **Scan for specific terms**
- **Find descriptive adverbs**
- **Judge something true or false**
- **Find the main point in long, complex sentences**
- **Analyze a line of argument**
- **Interpret charts**

Part 1 Soapy Smith

Use the photo and introductory note on page 171 to introduce the topic of the chapter. Review vocabulary related to crime and punishment.

Before You Read

1 Getting Meaning from Context. Page 172.
Review using context clues to guess the meaning of new words. Have students complete the exercise individually. Ask volunteers to explain how they decided on the meanings as you go over the answers.

Answers: 1. d 2. a 3. a 4. c 5. c

2 Skimming for Organization in Biography. Page 173.
Call attention to the common organization patterns for a biography. Have students point out similarities and differences between the patterns. Then ask them to skim the reading selection to determine which pattern is used. Have volunteers explain how they made their decision.

Answer: Organization 2

Read

Soapy Smith. Page 173. [on tape/CD]
Play the tape or CD as students follow along in their books. You may want to stop the recording as needed to check understanding and point out important vocabulary words. Listen a second time as students read along.

After You Read

3 Finding Examples to Support Main Ideas. Page 175.
Read the instructions and have students complete the chart about the character of Soapy Smith. Have students compare their charts in small groups. Go over any questions that arise the groups.

Sample Answers:
Good Side
1. made donations to charities
2. helped those in need
3. helped churches
4. started an adoption program for stray dogs
5. opened business
6. opposed violent methods

Bad Side
1. involved with gambling games

2. formed a gang
3. had a reputation for his con games
4. his gang was involved in robberies
5. had a protection business
6. had a telegraph business with no telegraph wires

4 Scanning for Compound-Word Synonyms. Page 175.

Go over the instructions as needed. Then have students look back in the reading for the compound words. Go over the answers.

Answers: 1. best-known 2. shoot-out 3. wide-open 4. townspeople 5. run-ins 6. overseeing 7. showdown 8. law-abiding

Making Connections

Have students research a folk hero or well-known person. Tell students to look for both positive and negative sides of the person. Students may want to present their information in a short oral presentation or in writing.

Answers will vary.

Talk It Over

Arrange students in groups of four to discuss the questions related to the life of Soapy Smith. Give the groups about 15-20 minutes to discuss the questions. Circulate among the groups, listening, and giving assistance as need. When all groups are finished, ask volunteers from each group to share the most interesting information and ideas from their groups.

Sample Answers:

1. Smith's Telegraph Office took money from people and said they would send telegraph messages, but the office could not send the messages because there were no wires. The business was selling something, but the customers were getting nothing for their money. I think there are businesses like this nowadays, but they are illegal. There are organizations that can check on businesses.

2. A con game is a trick or swindle. A person makes others feel confident. Then the person tricks or fools the person, usually taking money from the others. A protection racket is when a person or group promises to protect a business from dangers if the business pays a certain amount of money regularly for the protection. If the business doesn't pay for the protection, then the person or gang hurts the business. The con people are basically good. In con game movies, like *The Sting,* the people are organizing the con to pay back someone who hurt them. In protection racket movies, the people are usually bad and involved in other criminal activities.

3. Frank Reid was a surveyor and former Indian fighter who had helped settle the town of Skagway. He was one of the committee members who wanted to get rid of the criminals and crime in Skagway. He died in a gunfight with Soapy Smith. He was trying to keep Soapy Smith from entering a committee meeting. He killed Soapy Smith, but he was mortally wounded, too. He died 12 days after the fight.

4. If someone does nothing illegal, you still cannot tell if the person is good or bad. In most cases, they are probably good. But some people twist the laws or do things outside of the laws that hurt or take advantage of others. The people may not be breaking a specific law, but they are breaking the spirit or true meaning behind the laws.

5. Answers will vary.

Part 2 Eye Witness

Before You Read

1 Identifying Narrative Elements. Page 176.
Review the elements of narratives. Students can refer back to the information on page 156 as needed. Read together the questions about the characters. Then have students skim to find the answers to the questions. Go over the answers together.

Sample Answers:
1. The title tells you that someone saw a crime. He is male, with brown eyes, a thin mouth, moustache, and a tic. He is nervous, but a neat dresser. His name is Mr. Struthers. He is important because he is the eye witness. He wants to speak to the police lieutenant.
2. The narrative is told by one of the policemen. He is one of the characters in the story. He is the one who is talking to Mr. Struthers. He's a policeman working on a murder/mugging case. His name is Detective Cappeli.
3. Magruder is a old police officer who had been talking to Mr. Struthers.
4. The victim was Mrs. Anderson. She was the wife of the police lieutenant. She was standing on the corner waiting for a bus.

Read

Eye Witness. Page 178.
Read together the background information on the story and author, Ed McBain. Remind students to think about the question about who the murderer is as they read the story. Read the story as students follow along in their books. Ask comprehension questions and discuss vocabulary as needed. Reread the story and have students follow along again. Have students guess who the murderer is.

After You Read

3 Finding Descriptive Adverbs. Page 180.
Read together the instructions and go over the function of adverbs. Then, have students work individually completing the sentences with the adverbs of manner. Check the answers with the class.

Answers: 2. carefully 3. personally 4. warily 5. suspiciously 6. abruptly 7. quickly 8. wearily

Focus on Testing

Judging Something True or False
Read together the tips on true/false sections of tests. Then have students complete Exercise 1. Go over the items that are not immediately obvious.

Answers: 1, 8, 12 These seem tricky because there is some true information in the statements, but they require more thought to make sure all the information is true.

Have students complete Exercise 2. As you go over the answers, have volunteers correct the false statements.

Answers: 1. F 2. T 3. F 4. F 5. T 6. F 7. T 8. F 9. F 10. T 11. F 12. F

1. Mr. Struthers was a thin, neatly dressed man…
3. The victim who was murdered was the wife of the lieutenant.
4. The eye witness was important because he saw the murder. Eight other people claimed to have seen the mugging and murder.
6. The woman who was murdered was standing on a corner waiting for a bus.
8. Mr. Struthers didn't come to the police at once because he was scared that the killer would come after him.

9. Mr. Struthers said he had seen the killer clearly enough to …

11. Lieutenant Anderson never came to talk to Mr. Struthers because his wife was the victim and the other officers didn't want to bring him in until it was necessary.

12. At the end of the story, the identity of the murderer is not stated directly, but you are able to figure it out.

4 Solving the Murder. Page 182.

Read together the questions about solving the murder. Be sure students understand the vocabulary. Then, arrange students in small groups to share their ideas about the murderer and motive. Allow 10-15 minutes for discussion. Then ask volunteers from each group to share their ideas.

Answers will vary.

Talk It Over

This activity gives students a chance to express their ideas about mystery and crime stories. Arrange students in groups of four or five to discuss their answers to the questions. Allow 15-20 minutes for discussion. Have volunteers from each group report their ideas.

Sample Answers:
1. I think this is a combination of a crime story and a murder mystery. There is the mystery of who killed Mrs. Anderson. But it's also a crime story because the lieutenant is able to cover up his role in the murder.

2. The lieutenant was able to "get away with murder." He was able to do it because of his position and power in the police force. No one would want to accuse the head of the police department of a crime. Anyone who did would worry about what the head of the police would do to retaliate. In general, people in high government positions and very rich people (who can hire the best defense lawyers) can get away with murder. The normal people cannot.

3. Some detective and mystery stories are *Columbo,* Agatha Christie stories, *Sherlock Holmes, The Silence of the Lambs.* I like ones where there the emphasis is on the finding clues and putting the pieces together to figure out who did it.

4. Murder stories are popular because usually the focus is on how the good people track down the criminal and the criminal ultimately pays for the crime. People are also somewhat attracted by horrors. I think it makes them feel that they are fortunate not to be involved with such terrible deeds.

Part 3 Born Bad?

Before You Read

1 Surveying an Extended Nonfiction Reading. Page 182.

Read together the information about the organization of nonfiction readings. Call attention to the three kinds listed. Point out similarities and differences in the organization. Then ask students to skim the reading to determine which kind of organizational pattern is followed. Go over the answer.

Answer: 3

2 Finding the Main Point in Long, Complex Sentences. Page 183.

As you read together the instructions, ask volunteers to suggest examples of common connector words. Discuss the differences between main clauses and subordinate clauses. Call attention to the suggested steps for finding the main idea. Go over the example in item #1. Then have students work with partners to complete the rest of the exercise. Go over the possible answers.

Sample Answers:
2. Connectors: and, as it does
    Main idea: The reason one individual commits a crime has a lot to do with neurological differences and difference in upbringing.

3. Connectors: after
    Main idea: The NRC reported that the potential for violent behavior in individuals with identical experiences differs because their nervous systems process information differently.

    Main idea within main idea: The potential for violent behavior in individuals with identical experiences differs because their nervous systems process information differently.

4. Connectors: which
    Main idea: Certain hormones may help tip the balance from obeying to breaking the law.

5. Connectors: while
    Main idea: Each child is born with a particular temperament.

6. Connectors: which, such
    Main idea: Lead poisoning is the single best predictor of boys' disciplinary problems in school.

7. Connectors: after
    Main idea: Dr. David Lykken says that these traits correlate as strongly in twins who have been raised apart as in twins who were raised together.

Read

Born Bad? Page 184.
You may want to have students make predictions about the content of the reading based on the previous exercises, the title, and the photo. Read the selection as students read along in their books. Pause occasionally to ask comprehension questions and discuss vocabulary. Ask volunteers

to summarize the information that they read. Then read the selection again as students follow along in their books.

After You Read

3 Analyzing a Line or Argument. Page 188.
Tell students to complete the chart to summarize the main points for both sides of the argument. Students can compare their charts in pairs. Discuss and questions that arise.

Sample Answers:
Nature (genetics, biology)
2. crime is found in all cultures
3. 90% of violent crimes are by men who are more aggressive because of hormones such as androgens
4. biochemical imbalance may cause violence
5. genetic factors such as physical damage at birth, biological predispositions (a calm nervous system), low blood sugar are linked to violence

Nurture (environment, influence)
2. sex-role expectations
3. community standards
4. interactions among individuals
5. stable family can counteract trauma
6. lead-poisoning can cause brain damage

Main Idea: biology; more important than environment

Talk It Over

Allow students to discuss the answers to these questions in small groups. After 15-20 minutes of discussion, ask volunteers from each group report their ideas.

Sample Answers:
1. Answers will vary.
2. Some factors in the environment that cause crime are poverty, lack of jobs,

divided families, lack of education. If there is poverty, then people look for quick ways to get money. If there are no jobs, there is no stable way to get money to live. There is no organized pattern for daily life. In divided families, there is often a less stable atmosphere and environment for children to be raised. When there is a lack of education, people don't realize the opportunities for a better life or even a different way of life or how to obtain it.

3. The statement is false. Parents can teach and raise their children, but they cannot make all the choices for their children throughout their lives. Some children will end up making poor choices and could become serial killers, although if there was a stable family environment, I think the chances would be very slim.

4. In times of war or terrible stress, almost anyone becomes a criminal. The survival instinct takes over and people might do things to protect themselves and/or their families.

5. It sounds ideal to live in a world without crime. But it seems like the world would be very one-sided with little variety or intellectual challenge. You would need to program people like computers to live without crime. People have both good and bad in them. To have no crime, people would have to be just good, but then they wouldn't be "people."

4 Interpreting Charts. Page 189.

Explain the background information about prisons in the U.S. Clarify vocabulary as needed. Call attention to the two charts. Then have students answer the questions based on the charts. Go over the answers with the class.

Sample Answers:
Chart 1
1. The U.S. prison population has quadrupled.
2. It has quadrupled in 20 years.
3. Answers will vary.

Chart 2
1. This chart compares the prison populations of various countries. It also compares the prison populations as percentages of the general populations.
2. Japan, Italy, France, Germany, China, Brazil, the UK, Iran, and Russia have smaller percentages of their populations in prison than the United States. No country has a larger percentage of its population in prison than the United States.
3. Russia.
4. The reason suggested is that the United States imprisons people for relatively low-level drug offenses.
5. Answers will vary.

What Do You Think?

Using the Death Penalty.

This part of the chapter provides additional discussion possibilities related to capital punishment. You may want to read together this section before arranging students in groups for discussion. As students work in small groups, go around giving assistance as needed. After 10-15 minutes of discussion, have volunteers report to the class the most interesting points of their discussions.

Answers will vary.

Video Activities: Victim Support Groups

Before You Watch

Read the questions aloud and ask students to discuss their answers in small groups. Have students report to the class their answers.

Sample Answers:
1. A support group is a group of people who have or had similar problems and

meet together to help and support each other through the problems. There are support groups for different problems, such as: people who quit smoking, people who quit drinking, people who were criminals, people who were gamblers, people with young children. The purpose of the group is to help each other face their problems.

2. Some murderer cases might be: O.J. Simpson, Timothy McVeigh. McVeigh's punishment was death. I'm not sure if it was fair.

3. I think appeal means to ask for a new hearing or court case.

Watch [on video]

Ask students to read the questions to prepare them for the video. Then play the video and have them answer the questions. Review the answers together.

Answers: 1. c 2. the murderers
3. a, c, e 4. b 5. c

Watch Again [on video]

Point out the questions and explain that students need to watch carefully to find the answers. Replay the video and have students complete the exercise. Go over the answers with the whole class to summarize the information.

Answers:

Murder Victim: Ron Russe, Pamela Allen

Murderer: Linda Ricio

Relative of Murder Victim: Virginia Allen, Susan Fisher, Sammy Smith

Government Official: Kate Elke, Jim Roche

After You Watch

Assign this for homework. Tell students to use the questions to guide them as they prepare their summaries. Students can share their summaries with partners or in small groups.

Answers will vary.

The Physical World

Goals
- **Imagine the historical context**
- **Scan for facts and terms**
- **Identify the arguments**
- **Infer the values of another culture**
- **Read poetic prose**
- **Use more exact or colorful synonyms**
- **Discuss the symbolism of the circle**
- **Scan for important details**
- **Get meaning from context**
- **Complete a timed reading**

Part 1 Touch the Earth

Use the **In This Chapter** note on page 193 to introduce the chapter topic. Guide discussion of what students know about Native Americans, the animal kingdom, and environmental problems. You may want to make a list of vocabulary for reference as you go through the chapter.

Before You Read

1 Imagining the Historical Context. Page 194.

As you read together the instructions for this exercise, guide students to notice the title of the reading and the photo on page 195. Ask volunteers to suggest who the chief is and what group of people he might have led. Encourage volunteers to share information they know about the late 1800s in the United States and the conflicts that arose between the Native American tribes and the government of the United States.

You may want to bring in resource materials to familiarize students with Native Americans and their cultures. Then have students skim the reading to find the answers to the questions. Go over the answers with the class.

Sample Answers:

1. The chief of a tribe is giving a response to a representative of the U.S. government.

2. The U.S. government is asking the chief to sell the land.

3. The Native Americans were probably dressed in clothing made from animal skins. They were usually brown-skinned with black hair. The people representing the U.S. government were probably dressed in clothing made from cotton or wool. They may have been wearing army uniforms. They were light-skinned.

4. The Native Americans would probably not have had an academic education, but they were very knowledgeable about the land, the seasons, the wildlife, and plants. They lived simply, living off the land, making things they needed. They lived respectfully and as a part of nature. The other side respected formal education. They wanted the land for their own material benefits. They thought people had the right and responsibility to use the land and everything that was in nature.

2 Scanning for Facts and Terms. Page 194.

After students complete the exercise, go over the answers.

Answers: 2. treaties 3. Milk 4. Great Spirit

Read

Touch the Earth: A Chief's Response. Page 194. [on tape/CD]

Play the tape or CD as students follow along in their books. Ask comprehension questions and discuss key vocabulary. Listen a second time as students read along. Guide students to summarize the selection.

After You Read

3 Identifying the Arguments. Page 195.

Have students work in pairs to answer the questions about the reading selection. Then discuss the answers with the whole class.

Answers:
1. The Chief rejects the offer because money is not valuable to them. The land is priceless and it does not belong to him, the people, or to anyone.
2. He basically says that the land will be there forever—as long as the sun shines and the waters flow.
3. It explains that the land does not belong to men. The Great Spirit put the land there for people and animals. Selling the land would be selling the lives of all who depend on the land. That would be immoral.
4. The Chief offers to give the U.S. delegates anything that they can carry with them.
5. I think that the Chief's reasoning is very wise. Any changes in the land affect all the people and animals in the area.

4 Inferring the Values of Another Culture. Page 195.

As you go over the instructions for the exercise, review making inferences as needed. Allow students 10-15 minutes for discussion. Then ask volunteers to share their groups' ideas about the values of the Chief and his culture.

Sample Answers:
1. The things that are important to the Chief are the land, the water, the plants, and the animals. Everything in nature is important because they live from those things. They rely on nature for food, clothing, and shelter. They lived in close relationship with nature. Money and owning land is not important to him. His people did not need money. His traditions and beliefs were important. There is respect and appreciation for the land. The dominant values in North America are different. Most people are more concerned about people than about preserving or living in close contact with nature. But our society and way of life has changed, so we cannot live as simply as the Chief did over a hundred years ago.

Before You Read

5 Reading Poetic Prose. Page 196.

Discuss the use and meanings of images in poetic style as you read together the explanation. Call attention to the questions. Then ask students to skim to find the answers to the questions.

Sample Answers:
1. Black Elk refers to "in the old days when we were a strong and happy people..." It implies that now the people are not strong or happy.
2. He refers to the "power of the nation", "the people flourished", "the circle... nourished it", and "the wind gave strength and endurance".
3. He identifies his people to the birds. The tipis were round like birds' nests. The tipis were arranged like a nest of nests.

6 Scanning for Background Facts. Page 196.

After students have completed the exercise, go over the answers.

Answers: 2. Powder 3. Little Big Horn 4. Victoria 5. 30; 31 6. South Dakota

Read

Touch the Earth: The Meaning of the Circle. Page 196.

Play the tape or CD as students follow along in their books. Ask comprehension questions and discuss key vocabulary. Listen a second time as students read along. Guide students to identify the images used in the selection.

After You Read

7 Using More Exact or Colorful Synonyms. Page 198.

Call attention to the example. Then have students complete the rest of the exercise filling in synonyms. Have students check their answers.

Answers: 2. acquainted 3. roamed
4. configuration 5. a fundamental
6. flourished 7. nourished 8. endurance
9. whirls

8 Discussing the Symbolism of the Circle. Page 198.

Arrange students in pairs to discuss the questions. Go around the room, listening, and giving assistance as need. After 10-15 minutes, ask volunteers to share the most interesting information and ideas from their discussions.

Sample Answers:
1. When the Indian nation is strong, there is a flowering tree in the center of the circle. From the east came light and peace (like the sun rising). From the south came warmth (where the sun is most of the day). From the west came rain (like the winds that usually go from west to east). And from the north came strength and endurance (because the cold north weather). Knowledge came from the outerworld through the religion.
2. Black Elk used images from nature to show the importance of the circle. The sun and moon travel in circles. The sky is shaped like a circle. The seasons run in cyclical pattern. Birds' nests are shaped like circles.
3. Time also moves in a circle as in the seasons in the natural world and from childhood to adulthood in human life.

Talk It Over

Read through the discussion questions together before arranging students in groups of four. Give the groups about 15-20 minutes to discuss the questions. When all groups are finished, ask volunteers from each group to share the most interesting information and ideas from their groups.

Sample Answers:
1. I think Black Elk was a very wise and observant person. He probably watched things in nature and respected the importance of everything. Today people in leadership positions of major religions are considered to have spiritual powers. For example, the Dalai Lama shows it in his speech and his lifestyle.
2. The circle shows that everyone has an equal part and a voice in group decisions. No one is at the head or in front of the others. In other cultures, there may be a throne or special seat for the leader or head administrator. They may be different levels or rows for others in the decision-making group.
3. I think that it might be all right if the people are presenting the Native American culture in a respectful way for the purposes of educating others to alternative views on life. The movie *Dancing With Wolves* had a Native American theme. Native American baskets, pots, and blankets are popular design elements in homes, especially in the Southwestern United States.
4. Answers will vary.

Making Connections

If students are interested, have them research one of the topics listed that is related to Native Americans. Students can present their finding in writing or in an oral presentation.

Part 2 Migration and Homing

Before You Read

1   **Scanning for Important Details. Page 199.**
    Read together the explanation and background information about the next reading selection. Discuss vocabulary as needed. Then have students skim to find the answers to the questions. Go over the answers together.

    Answers: 1. Salmon 2. Sooty terns
    3. Golden plover

2   **Getting Meaning from Context. Page 200.**
    Call attention to the example and guide students to get the meaning from the context for the word "astonishing." Point out that students will need to find the word in context in the reading selection to guess the meanings. As you go over the answers, have volunteers explain how they derived the meanings.

    Answers: 2. d 3. d 4. b 5. b 6. d 7. c
    8. a 9. c 10. d

Read

3   **Migration and Homing. Page 201.**
    Read the selection as students read along in their books. Pause to check comprehension and to point out key vocabulary. Guide volunteers to summarize the main ideas of the selection.

After You Read

4   **Explaining the Mysteries. Page 204.**
    Have students complete the exercise, referring back to the reading selection as needed. Go over the answers with the class.

    Answers: 1. sense of smell 2. protection on islands from cats and foxes 3. celestial clues such as the sun, moon, and stars 4. sense the earth's magnetic field

Talk It Over

Arrange students in groups of four or five to talk about their own thoughts on animal instincts and experiments with animals. Allow 15-20 minutes for discussion. Ask volunteers to report their groups' ideas.

Answers will vary.

Focus on Testing

Doing the Easy Ones First
Read together the test-taking tips, clarifying as needed. Then have students apply the strategy as they do the practice test. Then arrange students in pairs to discuss their answers. Go over the answers with the whole class.

Answers: 1. b 2. c 3. b 4. c 5. a 6. c

Part 3 Down the Drain

Before You Read

1   **Rank Natural Disasters. Page 206.**
    Go over the list of dangers. Call attention to the example given for New York City. Then have

students work in groups of four or five to rank the disasters for three other cities that they know. Ask volunteers to share their groups' listings. Guide summary of the information.

Answers will vary.

Read

2 Timed Reading. Page 206.
Read together the instructions for the timed exercise. Remind students to preview the selection and look over the quiz questions before reading. You may want to have students read the selection on their own and complete the test. Then, read the selection and have students follow along before going over the answers to the test questions.

After You Read

3 Answering the Questions. Page 209.
As you go over the answers with the class, ask volunteers to point out lines in the reading selection that support their answers.

Answers: 1. d 2. b 3. b 4. d 5. a 6. c 7. d 8. b 9. d 10. c

4 Discussing the Timed Reading. Page 210.
Arrange students in small groups to discuss the speed and accuracy of their timed reading exercise. Have groups develop their own test-taking tips to share with the rest of the class as they answer the discussion questions.

Answers will vary.

What Do You Think?

Littering
This exercise provides additional discussion possibilities related to the earth and the environment. You may want to read together this section before arranging students in group for discussion. As students work in small groups, go around giving assistance as needed. After 10-15

minutes of discussion, have volunteers report to the class the most interesting points of their discussions.

Answers will vary.

Video Activities: Air Pollution

Before You Watch
Read the questions aloud and ask students to discuss their answers in small groups. Have students report to the class their answers.

Sample Answers: 1. a 2. a 3. respiratory problems, asthma, cancer

Watch [on video]
Ask students to read the questions to prepare them for the video. Then play the video and have them answer the questions. Review the answers together.

Answers: 1. a 2. The oil industry doesn't like the new rules because they will result in big price increases for fossil fuel products. 3. c

Watch Again [on video]
Point out the questions and explain that students need to watch carefully to find the answers. Replay the video and have students complete the exercise. Go over the answers with the whole class to summarize the information.

Answers: 1. c 2. b, d 3. meet; product; provide; cost that; afford 4. a, d 5. by 2007 6. for years after 2007

After You Watch
Assign this for homework. Remind students to use strategies for pre-reading and finding main ideas as they read their articles. Allow time for students to share their article summaries in small groups or with the class.

Answers will vary.

Together on a Small Planet

Goals

- **Recall information**
- **Separate fact from opinion**
- **Outline one view of friendship**
- **Find the theme**
- **Focus on development**
- **Express an opinion**

Part 1 Books

Introduce the chapter by reading together the **In This Chapter** note on page 213. Ask volunteers to name different prereading methods that they have learned. You may want to make a list of these for students' reference as they complete the readings in this chapter. Point out the topic of the readings: human existence and values.

Read

Books. Page 214
Read together the background information on the reading selection and the author. Allow students to share other information they know about Jorge Luis Borges. Remind students to use one or more prereading strategies. Then tell them to read the selection and complete Exercise 1.

After You Read

1 **Recalling Information. Page 215.**
After students complete the exercise, discuss the answers and have volunteers point out the parts of the reading that support their responses.

Answers: 1. b 2. c 3. b

2 **Small Group Discussion. Page 215.**
Arrange students in groups of four. Give the groups about 15-20 minutes to discuss the questions. Circulate among the groups, listening, and giving assistance as need. When all groups are finished, ask volunteers from each group to share the most interesting information and ideas from their groups.

Sample Answers:

1. The main idea of the essay is that books are very important and will not be replaced by any other form of communication. I don't agree, because I think the computer and Internet will be a challenge to books. People do not need to buy or go to libraries to get written information any more. So books will become less important.

2. I prefer to read a book. Usually I get more ideas and information about the characters or situation in the book version than in a movie version. The movie version tells one person's interpretation of the major points of a story. A book lets the reader decide for himself or herself what is important and how to interpret what the author wrote.

3. Answers will vary.

Part 2 Three Days to See

Read

Three Days to See. Page 216.
Use the background information to guide discussion of the challenges of the blind and deaf. Ask volunteers to share information they know about these physical challenges and about the life of Helen Keller. Encourage students to preview the reading selection and the exercises that

follow the reading. Then have them read the selection and complete Exercises 1 and 2.

After You Read

1 Recalling Information. Page 218.
Call attention to the directions and the example. Then have students complete the exercise. Go over the answers with the class.

Answers: 2. values 3. appreciation 4. deaf 5. blind 6. nothing (in particular) 7. interest 8. nature 9. granted

2 Separating Fact from Opinion. Page 218.
If needed, review the differences between fact and opinion. After students complete the exercise, have them compare their responses with partners. Discuss the answers with the whole class.

Answers: 1. F 2. F 3. O 4. O 5. O 6. F 7. O 8. O

Talk It Over

This activity allows students discuss the views on physical challenges and people who have disabilities. Students work in small groups talking about their answers to the questions. As students work, go around the room listening and giving assistance as needed. When students have finished the exercise, invite volunteers to share their answers and most interesting information from their discussions.

Sample Answers:
1. According to Helen Keller, her "disabilities" or "handicaps" allowed her to appreciate better things that others could see and hear. She used her other senses to experience things in nature. It sounded like she was more aware of and affected by things in nature because of her way of "seeing" and "hearing" things.

2. Answers will vary.

3. I think that we can learn a lot from Helen Keller. We should be very appreciative of the people and things that we can see and hear. We should actively look and listen to things around us. We should use the senses that we have to the maximum.

Part 3 Good Friend...Dogs, Sons, and Others

Read

Good Friend...Dogs, Sons, and Others. Page 219.
Read together the background information on Willie Morris and his essay. Call attention to the types of exercises that following the reading selection and suggest that students preview the reading by themselves. Then have them read the selection and complete Exercises 1 and 2.

After You Read

1 Recalling Information. Page 221.
After students complete the exercise, go over the answers with the class. Ask volunteers to correct the false statements to make them true.

Answers:
1. 1. T 2. F 3. T 4. T 5. F 6. T 7. F 8. T
2. A person should have a few steadfast friends.
5. The New York editor who wrote an article about the faults of his old friends betrayed his friends.
7. Death is not the end of friendship. Friendship is always in one's heart.

2 Outlining One View of Friendship. Page 222.
Review main ideas and identifying supporting details. Have students work with partners to

prepare their outline of the main ideas and supporting details or examples. Then have pairs share their outlines with others in small groups. Summarize as a class the main points.

Sample Answers:

1. A person can have only a few good friends.

   Friends can be male or female, pets, or children.

2. Loyalty is important in friendship.

   A good friend helps you no matter what you do.

3. Betraying a friend is very bad.

   An editor criticized all his old friends in print just to make himself look better.

4. Gestures can be as important as words in a friendship.

   During a baseball game, a white baseball player put an arm around Jackie Robinson, a black player who was being heckled by the spectators, to show his solidarity with Robinson.

5. Friendship goes beyond death.

   Willie Morris remembered a very good friend who had died. He remembered something that the friend would have said and it helped Morris complete a project.

6. Old friends are important.

   We have shared experiences which won't disappear even after years of separation.

Talk It Over

This activity allows students to talk about the author's main idea and their own feelings on friendship. Arrange students in groups of four. Give the groups about 15-20 minutes to discuss the questions. Circulate among the groups, listening, and giving assistance as need. When all groups are finished, ask volunteers from each group to share the most interesting information and ideas from their groups.

Sample Answers:

1. The main idea is that it is important for people to have good friends and to treat their friends well.

2. I think that the author is kind person who likes to be with friends and talk about things. I think he likes to do things with others.

3. Important qualities of a friend are honesty, faithfulness, patience, respect, intelligence, but not be condescending. A good friend should have a sense of humor and interest and curiosity about life.

4. I think that a person should have just a few good friends. A good friend knows you well and I don't think people want so many people to know them so well. Friendship is a private relationship.

5. Answers will vary.

Part 4 Poetry

Read

Poems. Page 223. [on tape/CD]

Use the information on page 222 to present the poetry and poets in Part 4. Review features often used in poetry. Have students preview the poems and then listen to the tape or CD as they read the poems. Encourage students to listen and read the poems several times.

After You Read

1 **Recalling Information. Page 226.**

Have students work individually on the exercise. Go over the answers.

Answers: 1. c 2. a 3. b 4. b 5. a 6. c 7. b 8. c 9. c 10. b

2 Finding the Themes. Page 228.

Have pairs of students consider the themes of the poems and answer the questions about the themes. Ask volunteers to share their ideas and support their responses with references from the poems.

Sample Answers:

1. All of the themes appear in the poems.

   Beauty: *Poem* by Ono no Komachi

   Death: *People*

   Freedom: *Caged Bird*

   Happiness: *Caged Bird, The Rubaiyat*

   Human nature: *People, Poem* by Ono no Komachi, *Poem* by Paavo Haavikko

   Love: *Poem* by Ono no Komachi, *The Rubaiyat*

   Suffering: *Caged Bird*

   Truth: *The Rubaiyat*

2. Happiness appears in 2 poems. Human nature is in 3 poems. Love is in 2 poems.

3. The poems tell us that beauty does not last. Death is final and it takes not just a person but all his thoughts and experiences. Freedom is important to those who don't have it. Happiness may be in simple things. Human nature is not always fair. Love is beautiful but does not last. Suffering may not be visible to others like the caged bird is suffering but he is singing. Not everyone wants the truth.

Talk It Over

Students can talk about their thoughts and preferences in the poems. After students have shared their views in small groups, ask volunteers to tell about the most interesting comments about the poems.

Answers will vary.

Part 5 Inaugural Address

Read

Inaugural Address. Page 229.

Read together the background information on John F. Kennedy and his speech. Allow students to share other information they know about Kennedy. Remind students to use one or more the prereading strategies. Then tell them to follow along in their books as you read the speech.

After You Read

1 Recalling Information. Page 230.

Have students complete the exercise, referring back to the reading selection as needed. Go over the answers with the class. Ask volunteers to correct the false statements.

Answers:

1. 1. T 2. F 3. T 4. F 5. F 6. T 7. F 8. F
2. Both sides should make plans to inspect and control arms.
4. These goals will not be accomplished in the first 1,000 days or even in our lifetime.
5. The common enemies of human beings are tyranny, poverty, disease, and war.
7. Americans should not ask how their country can help them. They should ask what they can do for the country.
8. People from other countries should ask what we can do for the freedom of man.

Talk It Over

Arrange students in groups of four or five to talk about their own thoughts on the Kennedy's speech and his ideas. Allow 15-20 minutes for discussion. Allow time for groups to report their ideas.

Answers will vary.

Part 6 Susana and the Shepherd

Read

Susana and the Shepherd. Page 231.
Read together the background information on this reading selection and author. Remind students to use one or more prereading strategies before reading the selection and completing the exercises.

After You Read

1 Recalling Information. Page 242.
Have students complete the exercise. Go over the answers with the class.

Answers:
1. b 2. b 3. b 4. c 5. a 6. a 7. c
Section 1: 8. b 9. c 10. b 11. c 12. b 13. b
Section 2: 14. a 15. c 16. b
Section 3: Juan's feelings change. He realizes that his dream of getting rich and returning home are not so important to him after his *abuelita* dies. He realizes that his older brother resents him. Ancelito explains how people from his hometown would feel differently toward him after being in America. Juan realizes that he can change his dream and he decides to try to bring his little brother over.

2 Expressing an Opinion. Page 244.
Students can complete this exercise individually. Then have students share their answers to the questions with partners. Ask volunteers to share their ideas with the class. Guide summary of the opinions.

Answers will vary.

Talk It Over

Have students discuss their thoughts on the main character and his experiences. Arrange students in groups of four or five to talk about their answers to the questions. Allow 15-20 minutes for discussion. Then ask volunteers to report their groups' answers and ideas.

Sample Answers:
1. At first, Juan Varra was homesick. He did not understand English, did not know anyone, and was unfamiliar with the land or customs. He overcame his problems by observing and working hard. He kept his dream, his goal in mind so it helped him realize the problems were temporary. It took several years for him to overcome his problems because he was quite isolated from others most of the time while he was taking care of the sheep in the mountains.

2. During the story, Juan changes. He wants to learn more English and he realizes that he likes Susana. Ancelito often explains things to Juan and he seems to realize that Juan is experiencing the same feelings that he had. Juan's grandmother died in Spain which affected him greatly. Juan's older brother sounded resentful in the letters. So Juan was more prepared for changing his dreams at the end of the story.

3. In my opinion, all of the characters are realistic. They are all people that faced difficulties in different ways. They all had some goals or dreams. They tried to help others. Family, land, and reputation were important to them.

4. Answers will vary.

What Do You Think?

Reading
Read together this section before arranging students in groups for discussion. As students work, go around giving assistance as needed. After

10-15 minutes of discussion, have volunteers report to the class the most interesting points of their discussions.

Answers will vary.

Video Activities: An Endangered Species

Before You Watch
Read the questions aloud and ask students to discuss their answers in small groups. Have students report to the class their answers.

Sample Answers:
1. A kangroo is a marsupial, an animal that carries its young in a pouch. They have very strong hind legs and tails and jump. They live in Australia.
2. d
3. No

Watch [on video]
Ask students to read the questions to prepare them for the video. Then play the video and have them answer the questions. Review the answers together.

Answers: 1. Tree kangaroos 2. Tree kangaroos don't jump. They climb trees. 3. b, d 4. It is found in the New Guinea forest. 5. c 6. b, c

Watch Again [on video]
Point out the questions and explain that students need to watch carefully to find the answers. Replay the video and have students complete the exercise. Go over the answers with the whole class to summarize the information.

Answers: 1. b, e 2. a, c, d 3. a 4. 2

After You Watch
Assign this for homework. Students can share their information about their endangered species in writing or in an oral presentation.

Answers will vary.

Reading Placement Test

Part 1 Determining Meaning and Usage from Context

Circle the letter of the best word or words to complete each sentence.

Example:

Public schools are forbidden to teach _____, whereas parochial schools are required to do so.

    a. religious

    b. spiritual

    c. mathematics

    (d.) religion

1. The puppy was very _____ with the children.

    a. calmness

    b. calm

    c. calamity

    d. calms

2. The father harshly _____ every boy who went out with his daughter.

    a. judge

    b. judging

    c. to judge

    d. judged

3. The patient was extremely _____ and had to be subdued.

    a. agitated

    b. agitates

    c. agitating

    d. agitate

4. Children who wish to _____ or achieve greatness must have drive and work hard.

    a. drive a car

    b. fail

    c. excel

    d. go home

5. **Poodles, German Shepherds, Golden Retrievers are different types of _____.**

   a. canines

   b. felines

   c. dogs

   d. a and c

6. **If you are having trouble logging onto the Internet you might want to check out your _____.**

   a. modem configuration string

   b. video monitor

   c. word processing program

   d. none of the above

7. **Spending time reading newspapers and _____ is a good way to keep up with current events.**

   a. historical novels

   b. ancient texts

   c. classic books

   d. other periodicals

8. **The enlightened ministers, Catholic priests, Jewish rabbis, and Buddhist monks _____.**

   a. belong to an ecumenical organization

   b. belong to the same denomination

   c. had identical religious training

   d. none of the above is possible

9. **She was a very _____ young child who could read university texts by the time that she was nine years old.**

   a. precocious

   b. illiterate

   c. developmentally delayed

   d. inadequate

10. **The mechanic was confident and felt that it was very _____ or plausible to get the truck repaired in a week.**

    a. unpredictable

    b. unrealistic

    c. feasible

    d. surreal

Part 2 Idiomatic Expressions

Circle the letter of the best meaning of the underlined idiomatic expression.

Example:

She wanted to leave under good terms and not to <u>burn her bridges</u>.

    (a.) make it impossible to return because of bad feelings

    b. destroy the bridges where she had traveled previously

    c. dynamite a bridge

    d. create bridges and avenues to the future

1. The mother told her son to be conservative and mindful of what he had since <u>a bird in the hand is worth two in the bush</u>.

    a. Birds fly away even when you have them in your hand.

    b. Birds are worth watching and loving: the more the merrier.

    c. It is better to hold onto something you own than to leave it unattended, and rush off to try to get something unknown.

    d. Always be conservative and never go after something new.

2. Carl's boss was against all of Carl's plans for improvement and <u>tied his hands</u>, which prevented him from doing anything innovative.

    a. was very proactive and supportive of Carl

    b. stopped him from working well

    c. put Carl into a psychiatric hospital where straitjackets were used

    d. Carl put his boss in a straitjacket

3. Cynthia's father adored her and <u>considered her to be the apple of his eye</u>.

    a. felt that his daughter could find lots of apples in the trees because she had such good eyes

    b. did everything he could think of to find apples for his daughter

    c. believed that his daughter needed to eat apples to improve her eyes

    d. believed his daughter was wonderful

4. George was mediocre at many different things; he was <u>a jack of all trades and master of none</u>.

    a. able to do many things that women could never do

    b. a master of many trades and did many things very well

    c. could do many different things, but none especially well

    d. a master of many things and did everything except one exceptionally well

5. She wanted to be promoted, but her hopes were <u>dashed</u> when her employer declared bankruptcy.

   a. dreams were fulfilled

   b. depression was deferred

   c. specific wishes were no longer possible

   d. life became joyful

Part 3 Scanning for Members of Word Families

Circle the letter of the best word to complete each sentence:

Example:

_____ is a noun meaning "a place that sells baked goods."

   a. Baker

   (b.) Bakery

   c. Baked

   d. Bakes

1. _____ is a verb meaning "to become more economical."

   a. Economize

   b. Economical

   c. Economics

   d. Economically

2. _____ is a noun meaning that "someone or something has grown fully or fully developed."

   a. Mature

   b. Maturity

   c. Maturing

   d. Matured

3. _____ is a verb meaning "to take an idea or concept and apply it in other situations."

   a. Extrapolation

   b. Extricate

   c. Extrication

   d. Extrapolate

4. _____ is a noun meaning "a person who tells jokes or funny stories."

    a. Comics

    b. Comedy

    c. Comedian

    d. Comical

5. _____ is a an adjective referring to "the cells of an unborn baby."

    a. Embryo

    b. Embryonic

    c. Embryos

    d. Amoeba

Part 4 Reading Comprehension

Reading 1

Have you ever thought about where you should sit on an airplane? It is important to book your seat early so that you can select a seat that best serves your needs. Individuals traveling in first class and business class usually need to think about whether they want an aisle seat or to sit next to a window or next to the bulkhead, or wall.

If you are stuck in the economy section of the aircraft you must still consider whether you want a window, aisle or a seat next the bulkhead. You must also take into account many different factors. You should decide whether or not you want to be in the front or rear section of the aircraft. The advantage of being near the front of the plane is that you will be able to board and deplane quickly. However, if you want to get an empty seat next to you, you should get a seat towards the rear, since people are assigned seats from the front to the rear. Please don't be discouraged if you end up with a center or middle seat since most airlines have middle seats that are a little bit wider than the window or aisle seats.

Based on the article, indicate whether each statement is true or false.

Example:

<u> F </u> **This short article was written by someone who is unfamiliar with air travel.**

    _____ 1. A bulkhead is not considered to be a wall.

    _____ 2. This article is about seat selection in both the economy and business or first class sections of an airplane.

    _____ 3. According to the article, if you are sitting in the economy section of a plane, you always want to sit towards the front of the section.

_____ 4. Seats are assigned from the rear of the aircraft forward.

_____ 5. You should be very upset if you get a middle seat.

Reading 2

Have you ever wanted to do something tremendous and earth shattering? You might think that you need to discover a cure for cancer, construct a huge monument, or be the first to fly around the world in a hot air balloon for your activity to count as being remarkable. Actually there are many very simple acts of kindness that can completely save a person's heart or life. My sister was recently touring Germany when she received some very devastating news. It was probably the worst news of her life. She was completely alone, in a strange land with no friends or family. A stranger, a big-sister-type figure, took her in and offered her both an ear and a cup of Earl Grey tea. That simple act gave my sister some of the courage that she needed to tackle her troubles. So the next time you want to do something great, simply take time to be kind to your fellow man or woman.

Based on the article, indicate whether each statement is true or false.

Example:

_F_ **We know for a fact that the author had a sister and a brother.**

1. ___ If something is earth shattering, it is unimportant.

2. ___ A cure for cancer is noteworthy.

3. ___ Simple acts are never great acts.

4. ___ The author's sister was given some very bad news while she was traveling.

5. ___ The stranger didn't offer the author's sister Earl Grey tea.

Reading 3

The Visually Impaired

Individuals who are blind, or those who are low vision, as well as those with less severe visual impairments, have benefited from a variety of key developments that have occurred in Europe and the United States during the past couple of centuries. Low vision refers to individuals who have very limited sight and it does not have anything to do with whether items are high or low to the ground. The effort to assist the visually challenged began in the latter 1700s, when a gentleman by the name of Victor Hauly committed himself to teach the blind. This noble act occurred after he witnessed people being paraded around as court jesters or struggling on the streets as beggars. Mr. Hauly founded a residential school for blind children that featured teaching children how to read with raised print. Following the precedent set by Mr. Hauly, Mr. Samuel Gridley Howe founded the world-renowned Perkins School for the Blind in 1821 in the United States. A variety of curricula and methods were both piloted and refined at the Perkins School. Anne Sullivan and her well-known pupil, Helen Keller, spent several years at the Perkins School.

A little over a dozen years after the establishment of the Perkins School, a French man named Louis Braille created the Braille's system. The Braille system, as it is now referred to, is probably the most successful method for teaching touch-reading and has survived the test of time. It is simple, utilizing a six-dot cell system, but should never be perceived as simplistic.

In the second half of the nineteenth century, one of the major advances for the visually impaired was not targeted at blind or very low vision children but rather at children who appeared on the surface to have "normal" vision. In the 1860s, a Dutch ophthalmologist invented or developed the Snellen chart. This was an important creation since it was and currently still is the most widely used device for visual acuity screening of school age children.

The first major development for the severely visually impaired took place between 1900 and 1913. Classes in public schools were opened in Boston, Chicago, and Cleveland for children who were blind or had low vision. This was a significant development since several local school systems began to recognize that the government had an obligation to provide education for children with severe visual impairments. Following the establishment of the public school classes east of the Mississippi River, other school systems followed suit.

The next trend to provide blind individuals with government supported services occurred in 1932 when the U.S. Library of Congress made talking books available to all legally blind individuals. Also in the 1930s, a California school district employed itinerant teachers to help students with visual impairments function in regular education classrooms. During this time period, also in the U.S., there was the inauguration of orientation and mobility services including a white cane to help people function in the community.

In the second half of the 20th century, the Perkins braillewriter was invented at the Perkins School for the Blind. The braillewriter made it possible for individuals sitting at simple machines to transcribe books into a touch-reading format. This increased literacy among those with severe visual impairments. It is hoped that the advances for the visually impaired continue well into the 21st century.

Circle the letter of the best word or words to complete each sentence.

Example:
The best title for this article could possibly be:

    a. Key Developments Impacting those without Visual Impairments

    (b.) Key Developments Benefiting those with Visual Impairments

    c. The Visually Challenged in Your Community

    d. People Who Help the Visually Impaired

1. Individuals with low vision _____.

    a. can only see things that are low to the ground

    b. have very minimal sight and can only see things that are low to the ground

    c. have very minimal sight

    d. none of the above

2. From the article, one can assume that Cleveland is _____.

    a. within 100 miles of Boston

    b. within 100 miles of Chicago

    c. east of the Mississippi

    d. all of the above

3. There have been certain residential schools founded for the blind. These include _____.

    a. the school founded by Mr. Hauly

    b. the school founded by Mr. Perkins

    c. the schools founded by Mr. Gridley Howe and Mr. Perkins

    d. the schools founded Mr. Hauly and Mr. Gridley Howe

4. All of the advances mentioned in this article took place in _____.

    a. Europe

    b. the United States

    c. the United States and Europe

    d. none of the above

5. The Braille system is _____.

    a. simplistic

    b. simple

    c. simple and simplistic

    d. neither simple nor simplistic

6. The Snellen chart is an important development _____.

    a. because it helped children who were completely blind and had no vision

    b. because it only helped low vision children

    c. because it helped to identify children who both have visual impairments and attend regular public schools

    d. because an ophthalmologist was involved in the creation

7. Although specific information was not given, one could assume that _____.

    a. Dr. Snellen did not invent the Snellen chart

    b. Mr. Perkins developed the Snellen chart

    c. Dr. Snellen invented the Snellen chart

    d. Mr. Perkins and Mr. Braille developed the Snellen chart

8. Talking books are only available for those _____.

    a. who are legally blind

    b. who can not be legally blind

    c. who have hearing aids and are legally blind

    d. who have any visual impairments, even minor ones

9. The white cane _____.

a. was designed to help the severely visually impaired students stay out of the community

b. was designed to keep the blind in residential schools

c. was inaugurated by the president of the Perkins school

d. was designed to help individuals with visual impairments function in the community

10. The Perkins braillewriter _____.

a. was the only invention in the 20th century that gave blind individuals access to books

b. was invented by Mr. Perkins

c. helped blind individuals have access to the printed word

d. none of the above

Reading 4

The Critic's Corner

This week, I will be writing about a topic near and dear to my heart as well as the heart of my children. Don't underestimate the power or value of children's literature or "kiddie lit" as it is sometimes referred. Many individuals find it surprising that children's literature, even books with little text, frequently encompass social themes that span from environmental studies to psychology or sociology. For example, "The Giving Tree" by Shel Silverstein is a very simple but elegant black and white picture book that tells the story of a boy and a tree that are mutually dependent upon one another. As the story unfolds, the man exploits the tree, while the tree remains gracious and benevolent towards the man. This book makes a powerful statement concerning man's disregard and downright callousness towards the environment.

Judith Viorst, a satirist, has written a charming picture book entitled "Alexander and the Terrible, Horrible, No Good, Very Bad Day." Her work, illustrated with black and white drawings, deals with the frustrations confronting a very young boy. Through the voice of a child, she reveals the emotional issues impacting children including sibling rivalry, parental approval, and unrealistic teacher expectations. This book is invaluable for those wishing to study the psychological makeup of young children, mainly boys but also girls.

Another book with a minimal amount of print worth checking out is "A Chair for My Mother" by Vera Williams. The story of a family who has lost all of their belongings in a fire is told, in part, through brightly colored illustrations accompanied by text. The community pulls together to get the family back on their feet. In addition, the family helps itself reach a goal through hard work and stick-to-itiveness. This book addresses some key sociological support systems, including the extended family and the community.

So the next time you are in a bookstore or library, take a deep breath and a moment to stop and browse the children's book section.

Based on the article, circle the letter of the best answer to each question.

Example:

What is the main topic of this article?

    (a.) Children's Literature

    b. Remedies for Social Problems

    c. Environmental Studies

    d. none of the above

1. How does the writer of the article feel about children's literature?

    a. The writer believes that it is a frivolous genre that should be dismissed.

    b. The writer believes that it has a great deal of merit.

    c. It isn't clear.

    d. The writer feels that it should be rejected from people's hearts.

2. In the first paragraph the words *mutually dependent* are used. In this context, what does *mutually dependent* mean?

    a. Both sides do NOT need one another.

    b. One side needs the other.

    c. Both sides need one another.

    d. Everyone is dependent upon the environment.

3. Which book deals with issues impacting the environment?

    a. "The Giving Tree"

    b. "A Chair for My Mother"

    c. both a and b

    d. none of the above

4. Which books are illustrated with black and white drawings?

    a. "The Giving Tree"

    b. "Alexander and the Terrible, Horrible, No Good, Very Bad Day"

    c. "A Chair for my Mother"

    d. a and b

5. According to the article, what can one assume?

    a. The writer has some familiarity with children's literature.

    b. The writer has no familiarity with children's literature.

    c. The writer doesn't want to read any more children's books.

    d. The writer checks out a lot of books from the library.

6. What did Judith Viorst, a mother herself, write?

    a. a book using a mother's voice

    b. a book only suitable for mothers to read

    c. a book using the "voice" of a child

    d. a book that could never have been written by a satirist

7. What was the psychological pressure, or pressures, mentioned in Judith Viorst's book?

    a. sibling rivalry

    b. parental approval

    c. teacher satisfaction

    d. a and b but not c

8. What happened to the family in Vera Williams's book?

    a. They suffered from a fire.

    b. They survived the fire.

    c. a and b

    d. none of the above

9. What does Vera Williams use to tell her story?

    a. only text to write her story

    b. only text to relay her message

    c. only illustrations to relay her message

    d. text and illustrations to convey her message

10. What is meant by the term *stick-to-itiveness*?

    a. lazy

    b. someone involved in sticky situations

    c. someone who cannot work hard

    d. someone who keeps on working until a goal is achieved

Name _____   **Date** _____

1. Match each word with its meaning. (5 points)

___ 1. blunt		a.	large size
___ 2. leisure		b.	popular in a large area
___ 3. assume		c.	small revolts and battles
___ 4. heritage		d.	about doing thing on your own with outside help
___ 5. inhabitant		e.	short and direct
___ 6. brevity		f.	shortness
___ 7. self-help		g.	suppose; believe
___ 8. widespread		h.	history and tradition
___ 9. vastness		i.	people who live in a region
___ 10. uprisings		j.	not working

2. Write *T* for true statements and *F* for false statements. (5 points)

___ 1. The climate of the U.S. is generally warm and humid all year.

___ 2. Most Americans enjoy traveling.

___ 3. For the most part, Americans are quite informal in their speech.

___ 4. Americans prefer to have household help.

___ 5. Most Americans enjoy showing off their homes.

3. Read the statements and decide which country is described. Write *C* for Canada and *US* for the United States. (5 points)

_____ 1. This country has two official languages.

_____ 2. The people in this country are more conservative than in the other country.

_____ 3. The people in this country generally express their emotions more openly.

_____ 4. This country separated peacefully from England.

_____ 5. This country has only one official language.

4. Circle the letter of the suffix. (5 points)

1. I love sitting in this chair. It's very comfort_____.

   a. -less   b. -able   c. -ful

2. Most people leave near other people, closer to civiliz_____.

    a. -ment   b. -ity   c. -ation

3. We saw a strange animal. We watched it with great curios_____.

    a. -ity   b. -er   c. -ment

4. Don't eat that plant. It might be harm_____.

    a. -less   b. -able   c. -ful

5. In some cultures, formal_____ is more important than it is in the United States.

    a. -ity   b. -ant   c. -ous

5. Write answers to the questions. Use complete sentences. (5 points)

1. Describe an American custom that seems strange to you.

_____

_____

2. How many official languages are spoken in your country? Do you think there are problems because of the official language(s)?

_____

_____

_____

3. What do you like about the United States? What don't you like?

_____

_____

4. What do you like about Canada? What don't you like?

_____

_____

5. Where would you prefer to live—in the United States or in Canada? Why?

_____

_____

Name _____   Date _____

1. Match each word or expression with its meaning. (5 points)

___ 1. kid	a.	slang expression for afraid
___ 2. chicken	b.	make a suggestion
___ 3. scan	c.	main idea
___ 4. skim	d.	read quickly for specific information
___ 5. cluster	e.	look at groups of words
___ 6. least likely	f.	was worthwhile
___ 7. give a hint	g.	read quickly to get a general idea
___ 8. assembled	h.	child
___ 9. thesis	i.	brought or put together
___ 10. paid off	j.	probably will not

2. Write *T* for true statements and *F* for false statements. (5 points)

___ 1. In informal writing, the sentences are usually short.

___ 2. When you preview a reading selection, you read the entire selection word by word.

___ 3. Previewing is a good way to review something that you read before.

___ 4. People need to understand and remember everything that they read.

___ 5. It takes practice to increase your reading speed and comprehension.

3. Read the types of questions. Write *O* if they are on objective tests and *E* if they are used on essay test. (5 points)

_____ 1. Fill-ins

_____ 2. Multiple choice

_____ 3. Thesis and arguments

_____ 4. Introduction and conclusion

_____ 5. True/false

4. Use the prefixes and root words to complete the sentences. (5 points)

	tell
re-	prepared
un-	view
pre-	familiar
	register

1. I don't know that story and I'm _____ with the author.

2. We have a test tomorrow, so I'm going to _____ the chapter and my notes tonight.

3. Mark forgot to study, so he was _____ for the test.

4. I didn't _____ for next semester, so I need to go sign up for classes now.

5. Maybe Anne will _____ the story for you. It's really funny.

5. Write answers to the questions. Use complete sentences. (5 points)

1. What are some things you look at as you preview a reading selection?

_____

_____

2. What are some light types of reading that you might skim?

_____

_____

3. What types of heavy reading do you have to do?

_____

_____

4. Do you prefer objective or essay tests? Why?

_____

_____

5. How do you prepare for tests?

_____

_____

Chapter 3 Quiz

Name _____   **Date** _____

1. Match each word with its meaning. (5 points)

____ 1. job sharing   a. survey

____ 2. adequate   b. wealthy

____ 3. radically   c. two people who each work part-time at one job

____ 4. breadwinner   d. a person who earns the money for a family

____ 5. trend   e. all that is needed

____ 6. poll   f. varying arrival and departure times at work

____ 7. advantageous   g. shown or pictured

____ 8. well-to-do   h. completely; to a large degree

____ 9. flex-time   i. tendency in one course of events

____ 10. portrayed   j. helpful; beneficial

2. Write *T* for true statements and *F* for false statements. (5 points)

____ 1. More than half of all the women with children work outside of the home.

____ 2. One income is always enough to support a family in the United States.

____ 3. Children are never cared for by family members any more.

____ 4. All companies and workplaces provide day care for their employees.

____ 5. As a result of working, the roles of husbands and wives have changed from the traditional roles.

3. Complete the sentences. Use the choices from the box. (5 points)

dating agency	marriages	barriers
personal ad	criteria	divorce

1. A man from Sydney, Australia met his wife by putting a _____ in a newspaper.

2. Many Russian women try to find a husband by applying for a file at a _____.

3. The _____ for selection are to have a good job, to know a foreign language, and to be blond and blue-eyed.

4. Embassies for some countries do not like _____ between citizens and foreign women.

5. Some countries try to set up _____ to limit migration from Russia.

4. Circle the letter of the correct word. (5 points)

1. Who is _____ care of the children?

   a. take   b. taking   c. taken

2. Many women are _____ in traditional fields, such as sales, education, and service.

   a. employ   b. employing   c. employed

3. There are many factors that _____ women to work.

   a. influence   b. influencing   c. influenced

4. During the Industrial Revolution, people _____ away from farms to larger cities.

   a. move   b. moving   c. moved

5. Fathers are _____ more time with their children now than in the past.

   a. spend   b. spending   c. spent

5. Write answers to the questions. Use complete sentences. (5 points)

1. Do you think it is good for mothers of small children to work outside of the home? Why or why not?

   _____

   _____

2. Which would you prefer—a day-care center or a nanny taking care of your children?

   _____

   _____

3. What type of person would be the perfect husband or wife?

   _____

   _____

4. What types of chores should women do?

   _____

   _____

5. What types of chores should men do?

   _____

   _____

Name _____   Date _____

1. Match each word with its meaning. (5 points)

___ 1. elite   a. to make someone angry

___ 2. eclectic   b. prosperity

___ 3. affluence   c. direct

___ 4. cuisine   d. combination of various styles or types

___ 5. downside   e. entering into the body

___ 6. intake   f. native

___ 7. widespread   g. the higher class people; the wealthy

___ 8. annoy   h. negative part

___ 9. indigenous   i. cooking style

___ 10. up-front   j. present in many locations

2. Write *T* for true statements and *F* for false statements. (5 points)

___ 1. It's better to eat simple foods than rich foods.

___ 2. All oils are bad for your health.

___ 3. In rich countries, people tend to eat more fruits and grains which are bad for their health.

___ 4. To find healthy food, it's important to know what is in a dish.

___ 5. There are no foods that help fight diseases like cancer or heart disease.

3. Complete the sentences. Use the choices from the box. (5 points)

ecotourism	locals	tourists
destinations	bargaining	begging

1. _____ bring money and problems to communities.

2. _____ was designed to protect the natural resources of scenic areas and allow visitors to see the natural beauty.

3. Many of the _____ don't want all the visitors and the problems they bring.

4. Some of the poor people were _____ for money and gifts from the rich visitors.

5. Some favorite _____ of backpacking travelers are Bangkok and Kathmandu.

4. Circle the letter of the correct word. (5 points)

1. Nutritionists have been _____ healthy foods from around the world.

   a. study   b. studying   c. studied

2. Scientists have _____ a lot of studies and information about healthy diets.

   a. produce   b. producing   c. produced

3. Many middle-income people are _____ weight.

   a. gain   b. gaining   c. gained

4. The change in diet may _____ the drop in some diseases.

   a. explain   b. explaining   c. explained

5. In Southern Italy, pasta, olive oil, garlic, and whole wheat bread _____ good health.

   a. provide   b. providing   c. provided

5. Write answers to the questions. Use complete sentences. (5 points)

1. What are your favorite dishes to eat?

   _____

   _____

2. Which do you think is the most healthful cuisine in the world? Why?

   _____

   _____

3. How does tourism help a community?

   _____

   _____

4. In what ways does tourism bring problems to an area?

   _____

   _____

5. What is a place that you would like to visit? Why?

   _____

   _____

Chapter 5 Quiz

Name _____   **Date** _____

1. Match each word with its meaning. (5 points)

___ 1. commonplace
___ 2. infrastructure
___ 3. vault
___ 4. dwarfed
___ 5. springing up
___ 6. bridging
___ 7. congestion
___ 8. sprawl
___ 9. suburbs
___ 10. assembly line

a. to move quickly or to jump
b. areas away from the city but not in the country
c. appearing
d. crowded together so there is no room
e. underlying foundation or framework needed
   for operations
f. present in large numbers
g. arrangement of workers and operations
   in a factory to put together a product
h. spreading out
i. made small
j. getting across

2. Write *T* for true statements and *F* for false statements. (5 points)

___ 1. There is little difference in technological development between the developing and developed countries.
___ 2. Developing countries are using modern technology and the Internet to improve life and business.
___ 3. It's possible for doctors and nurses to give medical advice by phone and computers.
___ 4. The Internet can help small and medium-sized companies advertise and reach markets far away.
___ 5. There is no hope to bring computer technology to developing countries.

3. Read the descriptions. Write *B* if they are about buses and *SC* if they are about street cars. (5 points)

_____ 1. They are run by electricity.
_____ 2. They were originally supported by oil, tire, and auto companies.
_____ 3. They contribute to air pollution, smog, and traffic.
_____ 4. They have made life better in cities in England and France.
_____ 5. They carried billions of passengers by the early 1920s.

4. Circle the letter of the correct word. (5 points)

1. People began to _____ the land outside of the cities.

   a. develop   b. development

2. This resulted in the _____ of the transportation systems.

   a. expand   b. expansion

3. When did John Wright _____ the electric streetcar?

   a. invent   b. inventor

4. The _____ of the streetcars was caused by several factors.

   a. disappear   b. disappearance

5. The government _____ of the highway system made traffic problems worse.

   a. construct   b. construction

5. Write answers to the questions. Use complete sentences. (5 points)

1. How often do you use the computer or the Internet? Why do you use them?

   _____

   _____

2. When is it useful to have a cell phone?

   _____

   _____

3. Which do you prefer to use—streetcars, buses, or subways?

   _____

   _____

4. Would you prefer to live in the city or the suburbs? Why?

   _____

   _____

5. Do you think everyone should have access to high tech? Why or why not?

   _____

   _____

Name _____   **Date** _____

1. Match each word with its meaning. (5 points)

___	1. executive		a.	friendly
___	2. multinational		b.	not enough; too small in amount
___	3. franchise		c.	pleased by praise
___	4. flattered		d.	involving many countries
___	5. startled		e.	type of food or products that are special
___	6. amicable		f.	not too expensive
___	7. absent-mindedly		g.	without thinking
___	8. inadequate		h.	surprised
___	9. affordable		i.	same store under one company name
___	10. specialties		j.	administrator or manager in a company

2. Write *T* for true statements and *F* for false statements. (5 points)

___ 1. Leopoldo Fernandez was successful because he was born in Spain.

___ 2. There were many pizzerias in Spain when Leopoldo Fernandez began TelePizza.

___ 3. Success came very slowly for TelePizza.

___ 4. Some nutritionists worry about Spanish people eating fast foods which are less nutritious than the Mediterranean diet.

___ 5. Fernandez believes that an immigrant feels the need to succeed more strongly than other citizens.

3. Number the events of "The Luncheon" in the correct order. (5 points)

_____ The narrator paid the bill and left a small tip which was all the money he had.

_____ The woman didn't want anything to eat, but then she had some salmon and caviar while the narrator ate the cheapest dish on the menu.

_____ Twenty years ago, a woman asked a writer to give her a little luncheon at an expensive restaurant in Paris.

_____ The narrator felt justice had been served when he saw how fat the woman is now.

_____ The woman had some champagne and asparagus and ice cream and coffee. She even ate a peach after all that.

4. Look at the italicized word. Then write a related word to complete the sentence. (5 points)

1. I like the *convenience* of fast foods. The pizzeria on the corner is a _____ place to eat.

2. The businessman *prospered* because of all his hard work. Now he has a _____ company.

3. We plan to *modernize* this old restaurant. We will install a _____ stove and refrigerator.

4. The new *manager* will start next week. He will be in charge of staff _____.

5. Do you like *mental* challenges? Do you have the _____ that it takes to solve business problems?

5. Write answers to the questions. Use complete sentences. (5 points)

1. What kind of fast foods have you tried or do you like?

   _____

   _____

2. What types of problems do people have when they start a business?

   _____

   _____

3. Would you like to have your own business? Why or why not?

   _____

   _____

4. Where do you prefer to shop—on the Internet, at a store, or from a catalog?

   _____

   _____

5. What advice would you give to a friend about managing money?

   _____

   _____

Name _____   Date _____

1. Match each word with its meaning. (5 points)

___ 1. enduring   a. keep track of; watch over

___ 2. diligent   b. grabbed; took control of

___ 3. strive   c. try hard; attempt

___ 4. eradicate   d. difficulties

___ 5. seized   e. perform better than others

___ 6. hardships   f. hardworking

___ 7. excel   g. lasting; continuing

___ 8. monitor   h. get rid of completely

___ 9. overwhelming   i. push down; keep from being known

___ 10. suppress   j. very great; overpowering

2. Write _T_ for true statements and _F_ for false statements. (5 points)

___ 1. Confucius was born into a rich and powerful family.

___ 2. He spent most of his life teaching.

___ 3. He believed that children should respect and obey their parents.

___ 4. For a long time, exams for government positions in China were based on knowledge of Confucian books.

___ 5. The Communist party in China based their government on the teachings of Confucius.

3. Read the statements about these remarkable individuals. Write _VF_ if they are about Vicente Fox and _KDJ_ if they are about Kim Dae-jung. (5 points)

_____ 1. He introduced an Indian bill of rights.

_____ 2. He won the Nobel Peace Prize.

_____ 3. He worked for peace and reconciliation between his country and a neighboring country.

_____ 4. He began a micro-lending program.

_____ 5. He plans to improve the economy and education in his country.

4. Add suffixes to the words to create nouns. Then use the nouns to complete the sentences. (5 points)

prepare	express	decide
invest	commit	assist

1. We need a lot of help. Any _____ you can give will be appreciated.

2. When the leaders make a choice, the _____ will be announced to the public.

3. This new company looks like it will be a success. Do you want to make an _____ in it?

4. We need to leave at 8:00. Do you need help with the _____ for the trip?

5. The team wanted to win, so the players made a _____ to each other. They promised to work long and hard to reach their goal.

5. Write answers to the questions. Use complete sentences. (5 points)

1. Why did Confucian philosophy remain widely accepted in China for many centuries?

_____

_____

2. Why did some governments prohibit or try to get rid of his teachings?

_____

_____

3. What are some characteristics of a good leader?

_____

_____

4. Who do you think is an example of a good leader? Explain why.

_____

_____

5. Many of the leaders in this chapter had difficult childhoods. What advantages or disadvantages do you think they had because of their childhood experiences?

_____

_____

Name _____   Date _____

1. Match each word with its meaning. (5 points)

___	1. spiral	a.	special; different
___	2. contemporary	b.	usual; typical
___	3. conventional	c.	not young but not old
___	4. fatigue	d.	the act of feeling sad about something
___	5. middle-aged	e.	traditional
___	6. heartlessly	f.	repeating
___	7. disappointment	g.	a winding curve like in a seashell
___	8. unique	h.	in a cruel manner
___	9. recurring	i.	present-day
___	10. old-fashioned	j.	tiredness

2. Write *T* for true statements and *F* for false statements. (5 points)

___ 1. Frank Lloyd Wright was interested in shapes and space.

___ 2. Wright designed buildings to make the owners happy.

___ 3. The Guggenheim Museum is famous for its beautiful paintings.

___ 4. People walk down a long circular ramp in the museum.

___ 5. Wright agreed to design the building because he liked modern art.

3. Read the statements about these creative individuals. Write *S* if they are about Steven Spielberg and *R* if they are about Roxana Robinson. (5 points)

_____ 1. This person's work is based on old-fashioned values.

_____ 2. This person believes you should create to free yourself.

_____ 3. This person creates sentences, scenes, and narratives.

_____ 4. This person creates visual images.

_____ 5. This person is a well-known movie director.

4. Circle the letter of the correct word. (5 points)

1. The man spoke to the woman in a _____ manner.

    a. friend   b. friendship   c. friendly

2. There was no _____ from the woman.

    a. move   b. movement   c. moving

3. The end of the story was a great _____ to me.

    a. disappoint   b. disappointing   c. disappointment

4. The main character was very _____ in his actions.

    a. prediction   b. predictable   c. predicting

5. What was the _____ of the young woman?

    a. occupation   b. occupied   c. occupying

5. Write answers to the questions. Use complete sentences. (5 points)

1. What do you think is the most beautiful building in the world? Explain why.

2. What is an example of a good story that you have read?

3. Would you like to be a writer? Why or why not?

4. What kinds of films do you enjoy?

5. Who do you think are more creative—men or women? Why?

Name _____   Date _____

1. Match each word with its meaning. (5 points)

____ 1. open-minded   a. looked for

____ 2. despair   b. liberal; willing to consider new ideas

____ 3. colleague   c. people not in a particular group

____ 4. sought   d. special treat

____ 5. foe   e. a sad state of mind

____ 6. outsiders   f. without being influenced by feelings

____ 7. objectively   g. a primitive or uncivilized person

____ 8. repulsive   h. co-worker

____ 9. barbarian   i. enemy

____ 10. delicacy   j. hateful; awful

2. Write *T* for true statements and *F* for false statements. (5 points)

____ 1. We all believe that our own culture is better than others, so we are all ethnocentric.

____ 2. Anthropologists study different cultures and try to make value judgments about the cultures.

____ 3. Some aspects of culture that anthropologists study are languages, clothing, and myths.

____ 4. In all cultures, cows and dogs are treated as pets.

____ 5. Most Americans who eat meat would prefer meat from dogs or horses.

3. Identify the story elements. Use the choices from the box. (5 points)

tone	theme	setting
characters	plot	conflict

1. _____ There were two waiters and an old man.

2. _____ It takes place in a café at about 2:00 in the morning.

3. _____ There's a sad and lonely feeling about the story.

4. _____ A customer is having a drink while the waiters talk. The customer finally leaves and the waiters close up the café.

5. _____ Some people have understanding and compassion for others and some don't.

4. Circle the letter of the correct word. (5 points)

1. What are the _____ between migration and the homing instinct?

    a. differences   b. different   c. differently

2. He has a _____ for hot, spicy foods.

    a. prefer   b. preference   c. preferable

3. An anthropologist tries not to make a _____ about another culture.

    a. judge   b. judged   c. judgment

4. They just _____ things as objectively as possible.

    a. observe   b. observation   c. observer

5. It's hard for me to _____ wearing clothes like that.

    a. image   b. imagine   c. imaginable

5. Write answers to the questions. Use complete sentences. (5 points)

1. What do anthropologists study?

    _____

    _____

2. What are some things about American culture that are distasteful to you?

    _____

    _____

3. What are some things about your culture that Americans might think are different?

    _____

    _____

4. What do you think is the most beautiful place in the world? Describe it.

    _____

    _____

5. What is culture shock? Have you ever experienced it?

    _____

    _____

Name _____   Date _____

1. Match each word with its meaning. (5 points)

___ 1. notorious   a. considered; thought carefully about

___ 2. eventually   b. really; almost completely

___ 3. best-known   c. mistakes

___ 4. run-ins   d. after a while

___ 5. overseeing   e. keep back; hold onto

___ 6. deliberated   f. meetings; encounters

___ 7. withhold   g. deciding confrontation

___ 8. slip-ups   h. supervising

___ 9. virtually   i. famous in a bad way

___ 10. showdown   j. most famous

2. Write *T* for true statements and *F* for false statements. (5 points)

___ 1. Soapy Smith was well-known and liked by everyone in Denver and Skagway.

___ 2. He made many donations to churches and charities.

___ 3. He set up many legitimate businesses in Skagway.

___ 4. Soapy Smith stole $2,700 from Frank Reid, a young miner in Skagway.

___ 5. Soapy Smith died trying to clean up the city of Skagway.

3. Complete the sentences. Use the choices in the box. (5 points)

eye witness	mugger	victim
confessing	line-up	case

1. Mr. Struthers went to the police station. He was an _____ to a terrible crime.

2. Detective Cappeli was investigating the _____. He was looking for clues and information.

3. The _____ of the murder was the wife of the police lieutenant.

4. A _____ had walked up to Mrs. Anderson and killed her.

5. Mr. Struthers didn't wait to look at the people in the _____. He was afraid of something or someone.

4. Add a suffix to the adjectives in the box to make them adverbs. Then use the correct adverb to complete the sentences. (5 points)

neat	stubborn	sudden
weary	suspicious	serious

1. She was very tired. She walked _____ towards the bus stop.

2. She heard a strange noise. She looked around _____.

3. _____, without warning, a man jumped out of a doorway.

4. The man wore dark clothes, but he was _____ dressed.

5. He bumped into her and grabbed her purse. The woman was not hurt _____.

5. Write answers to the questions. Use complete sentences. (5 points)

1. Do you enjoy detective or mystery stories? Why or why not?

_____

_____

2. What are some reasons that some people become criminals?

_____

_____

3. Why do you think there is so much crime in the United States?

_____

_____

4. Do you think the death penalty is an effective form of punishment? Why or why not?

_____

_____

5. Why do you think murder stories and murder cases are popular topics in books and films?

_____

_____

Name _____   **Date** _____

1. Match each word with its meaning. (5 points)

___	1. acquainted	a.	ability to go on
___	2. roamed	b.	wandered
___	3. configuration	c.	did well; grew strong
___	4. flourished	d.	separated
___	5. endurance	e.	goes round and round
___	6. whirls	f.	signs
___	7. astonishing	g.	shape; form
___	8. guideposts	h.	familiar with
___	9. isolated	i.	lined up; directed
___	10. oriented	j.	amazing

2. Write *T* for true statements and *F* for false statements. (5 points)

___ 1. The Chief of the band of Blackfeet believed that money is more important than the land.

___ 2. People and animals all depend on the land.

___ 3. The land gives life to men and animals.

___ 4. Anyone can own the land according to the Chief.

___ 5. The square was a special shape to the Indians.

3. Read the sentences and identify the type of animal. Write *F* for fish and *B* for birds. (5 points)

_____ 1. They use their sense of smell to migrate.

_____ 2. They use the stars and constellations to navigate.

_____ 3. They can sense the earth's magnetic field to find their direction.

_____ 4. They can recognize differences in the chemical composition of water.

_____ 5. They use the position of the sun to guide their migration journeys.

4. Circle the correct word. (5 points)

1. Farmers need to _____ 1,000 tons of water to grow one ton of grain.

   a. use   b. used   c. using

2. By the year 2021, many people in Africa will be _____ in countries with very limited supplies of water.

   a. live   b. lived   c. living

3. It is _____ that cities will grow by more than two billion people by the year 2025.

   a. project   b. projected   c. projecting

4. Today, some rivers are _____ biological deserts.

   a. become   b. became   c. becoming

5. There is hope because some rivers have been _____.

   a. restore   b. restored   c. restoring

5. Write answers to the questions. Use complete sentences. (5 points)

1. What images from nature do Native Americans use to show the importance of the circle?

   _____

   _____

2. How do you know that the Native Americans respected the environment?

   _____

   _____

3. Name a bird or fish that migrates. Where and why does it migrate?

   _____

   _____

4. Why is there a world water crisis?

   _____

   _____

5. What other environmental problems need to be solved?

   _____

   _____

Name _____   **Date** _____

1. Match each word with its meaning. (5 points)

___	1. diverse	a.	stress; point out the importance
___	2. emphasize	b.	the lessening of strength or usefulness of something
___	3. impairment	c.	a manner worth of respect
___	4. genuine	d.	brightly
___	5. betrayal	e.	plan in an orderly way
___	6. vividly	f.	different
___	7. trill	g.	make a serious effort to do something
___	8. formulate	h.	sing
___	9. endeavor	i.	the act of being disloyal
___	10. dignity	j.	real

2. Write *T* for true statements and *F* for false statements. (5 points)

___ 1. Most people take life for granted.

___ 2. Helen Keller was probably sad in the forest because she was blind.

___ 3. People should appreciate their senses.

___ 4. Willie Morris thinks that it is important to have only a few good friends.

___ 5. Pets can never be as good of a friend as a person can.

3. Write the theme next to the lines of poetry. Use the choices from the box. (5 points)

freedom	beauty	death	happiness
love	truth	suffering	

_____ 1. "They perish. They cannot be brought back. The secret worlds are not regenerated."

_____ 2. "The single flower which blossoms in the fickle heart of man."

_____ 3. "The caged bird sings…of things unknown but longed for still."

_____ 4. "To each his world is private and in that world one excellent minute."

_____ 5. "But a bird that stalks down his narrow cage can seldom see through his bars of rage his wings are clipped and his feet are tied…"

4. Number the events of Susana and the Shepherd in the correct order. (5 points)

_____ The sheep and land are different and Juan feels homesick.

_____ Juan meets Susana but he continues to hold onto his dream.

_____ Juan travels from the Spanish Pyrenees for a job in California because of his dream to own his own land and herd of sheep.

_____ After the death of his grandmother and some letters from his older brother, Juan believes that he can change his dream.

_____ Ancelito meets Juan and gives him a brief orientation before Juan begins herding the sheep.

5. Write answers to the questions. Use complete sentences. (5 points)

1. What are the most important qualities of a good friend?

_____

_____

2. How can citizens of a country can help their country?

_____

_____

3. How can citizens of the world work together for the freedom of man?

_____

_____

4. In what ways did Juan change in the story Susana and the Shepherd?

_____

_____

5. What types of reading do you enjoy the most—essays, poetry, nonfiction, fiction? Why?

_____

_____

Placement Test Answer Key

Part 1 Determining Meaning and Usage from Context

Example: d

1. b
2. d
3. a
4. c
5. d
6. a
7. d
8. a
9. a
10. c

Part 2 Idiomatic Expressions

Example: a

1. c
2. b
3. d
4. c
5. c

Part 3 Scanning for Members of Word Families

Example: b

1. a
2. b
3. d
4. c
5. b

Part 4 Reading Comprehension

Reading 1
Example: F

1. F
2. T
3. F
4. F
5. F

Reading 2
Example: F

1. F
2. T
3. F
4. T
5. F

Reading 3
Example: b

1. c
2. c
3. d
4. c
5. b
6. c
7. c
8. a
9. d
10. c

Reading 4
Example: a

1. b
2. c
3. a
4. d
5. a
6. c
7. d
8. c
9. c
10. d

Answer Keys for Chapter Quizzes

Chapter 1

1.
1. e
2. j
3. g
4. h
5. i
6. f
7. d
8. b
9. a
10. c

2.
1. F
2. T
3. T
4. F
5. T

3.
1. C
2. C
3. US
4. C
5. US

4.
1. b
2. c
3. a
4. c
5. a

5. Answers will vary.

Chapter 2

1.
1. h
2. a
3. d
4. g
5. e
6. j
7. b
8. i

9. c
10. f

2.
1. T
2. F
3. F
4. F
5. T

3.
1. O
2. O
3. E
4. E
5. O

4.
1. unfamiliar
2. review
3. unprepared
4. preregister
5. retell

5. Answers will vary.

Chapter 3

1.
1. c
2. e
3. h
4. d
5. i
6. a
7. j
8. b
9. f
10. g

2.
1. T
2. F
3. F
4. F
5. T

3.
1. personal ad
2. dating agency
3. criteria
4. marriages
5. barriers

4.
1. b
2. c

Answer Keys

3. a
4. c
5. b

5. Answers will vary.

Chapter 4

1.
1. g
2. d
3. b
4. i
5. h
6. e
7. j
8. a
9. f
10. c

2.
1. T
2. F
3. F
4. T
5. F

3.
1. Tourists
2. Ecotourism
3. locals
4. begging
5. destinations

4.
1. b
2. c
3. b
4. a
5. a

5. Answers will vary.

Chapter 5

1.
1. f
2. e
3. a
4. i
5. c
6. j
7. d
8. h
9. b
10. g

2.
1. F
2. T
3. T
4. T
5. F

3.
1. SC
2. B
3. B
4. SC
5. SC

4.
1. a
2. b
3. a
4. b
5. b

5. Answers will vary.

Chapter 6

1.
1. j
2. d
3. i
4. c
5. h
6. a
7. g
8. b
9. f
10. e

2.
1. F
2. F
3. F
4. T
5. T

3. 4, 2, 1, 5, 3

4.
1. convenient
2. prosperous
3. modern
4. management
5. mentality

5. Answers will vary.

Chapter 7

1.
1. g
2. f
3. c
4. h
5. b
6. d
7. e
8. a
9. j
10. i

2.
1. F
2. T
3. T
4. T
5. F

3.
1. VF
2. KDJ
3. KDJ
4. VF
5. VF

4.
1. assistance
2. decision
3. investment
4. preparation
5. commitment

5. Answers will vary.

Chapter 8

1.
1. g
2. i
3. b
4. j
5. c
6. h
7. d
8. a
9. f
10. e

2.
1. T
2. F
3. F
4. T
5. F

3.
1. S
2. R
3. R
4. S
5. S

4.
1. a c
2. b
3. c
4. b
5. a

5. Answers will vary.

Chapter 9

1.
1. b
2. e
3. h
4. a
5. i
6. c
7. f
8. j
9. g
10. d

2.
1. T
2. F
3. T
4. F
5. F

3.
1. characters
2. setting
3. tone
4. plot
5. theme

4.
1. a
2. b
3. c

4. a
5. b

5. Answers will vary.

Chapter 10

1.
1. i
2. d
3. j
4. f
5. h
6. a
7. e
8. c
9. b
10. g

2.
1. F
2. T
3. F
4. F
5. F

3.
1. eye witness
2. case
3. victim
4. mugger
5. line-up

4.
1. wearily
2. suspiciously
3. Suddenly
4. neatly
5. seriously

5. Answers will vary.

Chapter 11

1.
1. h
2. b
3. g
4. c
5. a
6. e
7. j
8. f
9. d
10. i

2.
1. F
2. T
3. T
4. F
5. F

3.
1. F
2. B
3. B
4. F
5. B

4.
1. a
2. c
3. b
4. c
5. b

5. Answers will vary.

Chapter 12

1.
1. f
2. a
3. b
4. j
5. i
6. d
7. h
8. e
9. g
10. c

2.
1. T
2. F
3. T
4. T
5. F

3.
1. death
2. love/happiness
3. freedom
4. truth
5. suffering

4. 3, 4, 1, 5, 2

5. Answers will vary.